WHO
SPEAKS
FOR THE
CHURCH?

WHO
SPEAKS
FOR THE
CHURCH?

A Critique of the 1966 Geneva Conference on Church and Society

Paul Ramsey

ABINGDON PRESS • NASHVILLE AND NEW YORK

WHO SPEAKS FOR THE CHURCH?

Copyright © 1967 by Abingdon Press

Library of Congress Catalog Card Number: 67-24331

SET UP, PRINTED, AND BOUND BY THE
PARTHENON PRESS, AT NASHVILLE,
TENNESSEE, UNITED STATES OF AMERICA

To my daughter Janet's daughter

ARLETTE CYBÈLE COOPER

ON HER FIRST BIRTHDAY

She will grow up to comprehend better things

ACKNOWLEDGMENTS

The concluding section of this volume reprints an earlier and briefer statement of my proposal concerning ecumenical social ethics. This was in an article entitled "The Church and the Magistrate" published in *Christianity and Crisis*, June 28, 1965, pp. 136-40. It is reprinted here with the permission of the editor.

For comparison with the text of the 1966 Geneva Report, portions of the official reports of the 1937 Oxford Conference and the 1948 Amsterdam Assembly are reprinted in the Appendix.

The report of the Geneva Conference has now been published by the World Council of Churches, Geneva, 1967, under the title, *Christians in the Technical and Social Revolutions of Our Time: World Conference on Church and Society: Official Report.*

I am indebted to the following persons who read the

7

manuscript of this volume, in whole or in part, and gave me the benefit of their criticisms: Professor William Lazareth of the Lutheran Theological Seminary in Philadelphia; Professor Ralph Potter of the Harvard Divinity School and the Center for Population Studies at Harvard University; Professor Thomas Derr of the Department of Religion at Smith College; the Rev. Alan Brockway, Editor of *Concern;* Dr. William Loos, President, Council on Religion and International Affairs; and the Rev. Dr. Alan Geyer, Director of International Relations for the Council for Christian Social Action of the United Church of Christ. It is unimportant to what extent any of these persons agrees or disagrees with any of the theses of this volume; for these the author is responsible. But it was helpful that they judged that there were some things herein worth attending to.

CONTENTS

INTRODUCTION

This small volume is a *partial* critique of the 1966 Geneva Conference on Church and Society, and of the methods and goals of the World Council of Churches, the National Council of Churches, and their member denominations when they deal with urgent social and political questions.

I say this is a *partial* critique, because in what follows I have naturally said a great deal more (in illustration of my thesis) about questions of justice in war and peace, with which I have been concerned in recent years in my professional capacity as one who does Christian ethics, than about other issues in ecumenical ethics. Someone else would have made a different selection of the issues. Still, in regard to the subjects I have taken up for consideration, I venture to believe that there may be in the detailed unpacking of them some small contribution made to the analysis and history of ecumenical ethics in our times.

This is, secondly, a partial critique of the current fashion in ecumenical social ethics because I say a good deal more about what I believe to be wrong with the procedures, the aspired goals, and the results of "Church and Society" conferences and pronouncements than I do about their strengths. I ask that this be noted, and held in mind. In what follows, I do not undertake a complete appraisal of the social and political ethics that has to date been achieved in the older (non-Roman Catholic) ecumenical movement. That is the task of a more synoptic account than is proposed here.

I was present at the Geneva Conference on Church and Society through the courtesy and initiative of Professor John Bennett, President of Union Theological Seminary in New York City, and at the invitation of the Rev. Paul Abrecht, the organizing secretary of the conference. While not a full or official participant, I was given the status of "co-opted staff," which enabled me to engage as a nonvoting member in the discussions of the subsection to which I was assigned, and in the section meetings. With no practical possibility or right to participate in the debates of the plenary sessions of the conference, I nevertheless was extended the privilege of attending plenary meetings, debates, and addresses. Beyond this, there were even more valuable opportunities for discussion of issues over meals and in the halls of the Ecumenical Center and at the Hôtel Intercontinental.

For these privileges I am very grateful. The fact that views I had already begun to formulate concerning ecumenical social ethics[1] were, in the main, confirmed and strengthened by my experiences at Geneva is no fault of my hosts. In truth, I suspect that various "styles," programs, and convictions about the way churchmen should be doing social and political ethics today, and everyone's approval, disapproval, or doubts about the current mode, were only upheld by Geneva; and that in this the author is no exception.

In what follows I speak of the "social action *curia*"[2] and of a "Church and Society syndrome." This is intended descriptively, and not pejoratively. Perhaps, however, here at the beginning I should say what I mean by this syndrome. I mean the passion for numerous particular pronouncements on policy questions to the consequent neglect of basic decision- and action-oriented principles of ethical and political analysis. There is no doubt that the churches and churchmen need to engage, whenever they meet, in the clarification and development of an ecumenical ethics for our own mutual guidance, for the guidance of other church members, our fellow citizens, and political leaders alike, who are seeking to know what to do in the face of urgent contemporary problems. Still this emphasis upon reaching some sort of agreement upon specific pronouncements or conclusions (correct or incorrect, competent or incompetent ones) is misleading. It is misleading in that we both want and yet do not want to be speaking for the church to the world and to the churches (and this is oppressive to the consciences of equally sincere Christians who prudently disagree). It is misleading in the further sense that it leads us away from the clarification of the meaning of every ingredient of Christian responsibility that is most needed at this hour. This can, I think, be seen by the "flight from justice" in the doing of ecumenical ethics from the Oxford to the Amsterdam to the Geneva Conference.[3] It is evidenced also by the deflection of ecumenical ethics all the more into specific policy questions when it was discovered that the church hardly knew its own mind, or has a common mind, about the meaning of "a responsible society."

In proposing a reversal of these priorities, and a return to primary emphasis upon the discussion of fundamental questions that churchmen as such are supposed to know something about for (it may be) the instruction of the

13

nations, I appeal to developments in "Faith and Order" since Lund and to the Second Vatican Council. The appeal is both to better deliberative procedures and to a crucial difference in the aspired goals and statements. I do not say that "Faith and Order" or the Vatican Council is a perfect model, or that the latter is on all fours with anything that is possible in assemblies of the older (non-Roman Catholic) ecumenical movement. These are only models with which to compare the Church and Society syndrome. If they are in many respects not even good models, then better ones will have to be invented, if ever a critical and charitable intelligence can bring under scrutiny what we have lately been doing (and consequently failing to do) in ecumenical ethics.

My positive proposal is very much like John Bennett's in his 1961 presidential address to the American Society of Christian Ethics. Speaking on "Principles and the Context," Bennett explained his concern for action-oriented principles by saying that

As a teacher of students who are expecting to preach, who are not themselves to be makers of political or social policy, I have been interested in finding out what kind of ethical guidance it is appropriate for ministers to include in preaching or for the church as church to provide its members. Also, I have often been involved in the preparation of ecumenical reports which must have some relevance for many situations without providing all that is necessary for decision in any situation. . . . It is important to have some designation of objectives or judgments which have a particular reference to our concrete situation, which are determiners of policy and yet which are not identical with the most concrete policy which is the immediate guide to action. . . . The corporate teaching of the church on controversial social issues is seldom more specific than the projection of so-called "middle axioms" [4] but if these do become a part of the mind of the church it becomes possible for it more effectively to encourage its members and many voluntary groups to experiment with the support of specific policies.

The latter is the province of political prudence. Of late, however, ecumenical social action pronouncements have presumed to encompass the prudence of churchmen in their capacities as citizens. It has been easier to arrive at specific recommendations and condemnations after inadequate deliberation than to penetrate to a deeper and deeper level the meaning of Christian responsibility—leaving to the conscience of individuals and groups of individuals both the task and the freedom to arrive at specific conclusions through untrammeled debate about particular social policies. Radical steps need to be taken in ecumenical ethics if ever we are to correct the pretense that we are makers of political policy and get on with our proper task of nourishing, judging, and repairing the moral and political *ethos* of our time.

To pay attention to the distinctive and basic features of Christian social ethics would as a consequence lead to much greater reticence in reaching particular conclusions. It would make for a proper hesitation in faulting the consciences of our fellow Christians, or in instructing them too narrowly, by pronouncements issued by official and semiofficial conferences of churchmen on policy questions concerning which there may be legitimate differences in practical, prudential judgment. To eschew the latter would also focus our attention upon the former, more fundamental work of clarifying the church's address to the world.

In any case, there can be no doubt that this distinction is currently violated both in pulpit and whenever churchmen get together as churchmen. "Liberals" discern this to be the case in the sermons and assemblies of evangelical conservatives. "Evangelicals" discern this to be the case in the sermons and assemblies of liberals. They are both correct.

15

The only way to go beyond or rise above this fruitless combat is to recall that an ecumenical Christian ethics must be the clarification of the message of the church concerning the meaning of Christian life in the contemporary world, even as theology is the clarification of the message of the church concerning the faith by which we live.

In what follows, I attempt to chart a course between pious generalities and particular policy conclusions. It would seem obvious that there must be such a way to go in the social thought of the churches—unless we are to deny that there is an alternative that needs to be stated in between saying "Be brave" and saying "Bravery must mean *this.*" My wording for a possible class of church teachings that goes between or beyond a forced choice of either ethical generalities or prudential specifics is "decision-oriented on action-oriented (relevant)" social and political analysis. I speak of "direction" in contrast to particular "directives" addressed to the world's urgent problems. Our quest should be to find out whether there is anything especially Christian and especially important that churchmen *as such* may have to say in the public forum concerning the direction of public policy— not directives for it. I respectfully ask the reader to pay attention to what is said under these heads, and that this little tract be not dismissed out of hand by anyone who may now believe that the only alternative to policy-making exercises would be to fall back on the utterance of socially irrelevant generalities when speaking for the church to the world of today.

At this point some may say that the distinction between a direction for action and a directive of the action, or between decision- and action-oriented church teachings and a specific pronouncement, is in a sense only a relative distinction. This, of course, is true; but this distinction can nevertheless be drawn, and it must be drawn if Christians are to find their proper voice.

Then, some may say, this critique of ecumenical social ethics is directed against an *abuse* of a basically correct undertaking in and among the churches. My thesis, however, is that the *abusus* (policy-directives) has become *usus*—it has become the fashion—and that one will not sense the strength of the case for a radical reformation in the aims of church social teachings unless he begins by acknowledging this to be true. The *abusus* amounting to *usus* has two correlated aspects: (1) The *directions* for decision and action (in which still consist the *strengths* of such documents as the Geneva Report) have too few Christian warrants, and there are other such warrants or Christian perspectives upon life in this world that would have entailed *additional* directions supplementing and *correcting* the action-relevant Christian social teaching currently addressed to the world; and (2) our "sins" of omission in saying all that needs to be said in this fundamental middle area about man's life in the world arise from our hurry to commit a particular pronouncement which, whether correct or not, is the proper work of social, economic, and political wisdom (prudence).

Some readers of the present volume may be inclined to say that this is a *partial* critique in a further and bad sense of that word. It may be charged that the criticism mounted herein against the excessively particular, specific pronouncements addressed by churches and churchmen (meeting as such) to urgent public questions, is partisan in the additional sense that I simply find myself in disagreement with a number of the specific recommendations and incriminations that have lately been forthcoming.

Perhaps a sort of preemptive reply should be given to this objection. It is certainly fair to say that every one of us should acknowledge the possible bias that may come from the particular opinions we hold on controversial public questions and which we may want the churches and our fellow churchmen to support also. But in correcting for probable bias, the present writer may be in a fortunate position, since I can honestly disclaim any desire to have the particular judgments and prudential political conclusions I believe to be correct, or possibly correct, in public policy today substituted for any of the particular conclusions on these questions that have lately been made in ecumenical social ethics. It might also be observed, wryly, that many a reader will surely agree, upon becoming acquainted with these opinions, that this is the last thing that should be wanted!

Agreement or disagreement with a certain set of specific church pronouncements on social and political questions is purely fortuitous in relation to the principal question this volume raises. The question is whether and how far such judgments may be deduced or adduced—or in any other way entailed—by the shared affirmations of *Christian* social ethics *as such*.

It cannot, of course, be denied that objection to the specificity and number of NCC and WCC resolutions may be only a cloak for disagreement with these particular conclusions, and not with others. At the same time, it is equally true that the defenses made of the aspired goal and the practice of offering specific advice on all sorts of complex subjects also may only cloak a passionate conviction that the religious forces should be "mobilized" behind one or another particular recommendation in which a person happens to believe.

Anyone who defends as a general matter the current procedure and intention of ecumenical ethics and who in the main agrees with the patterns of specifics that have

18

lately been forthcoming is in at least as much of a quandary in dealing with his biases as I am. It is fair, I think, to ask that this be noted—for the sake of beginning a serious, self-critical scrutiny of what we have been doing and are continuing to do as churches and churchmen in the older ecumenical movement in regard to Church and Society.

None of us knows what will be the shape of ecumenical social ethics once we get down to the business of saying to one another everything that can and may and must be said, and to one another and to the world no more than can properly be said, upon public questions in the light of our knowledge of God and man, ethics and politics, in Christ Jesus. The rest is certainly not a matter of indifference. The world's unsolved and insoluble problems are too important for that to be said. But the specific solution of urgent problems is the work of political prudence and worldly wisdom. In this there is room for legitimate disagreement among Christians and among other people as well in the public domain—which disagreement ought to be welcomed and not led one way toward specific conclusions. We need to sort out what may be action-oriented or policy-oriented statements that fall within the *de jure* competence of the churches and churchmen to enunciate to anyone who has the ears to hear. However relevant, these will be distinct from public policy formation in which we with all men engage as citizens—inspired by our faith and ethics no doubt, but with no special guidance that should either bind or ease the consciences of men in venturing the actions that shape our common future.

There is urgent need, and now is the time, for those of us who love the church, and who share in striving for an ecumenical ethics in the world of today, to engage in a probing examination of what we are doing (and consequently failing to do) in formulating the church's address to the world. My thesis is that, if such an examination is undertaken, we will no longer be able to speak and act as if there is a closer identification between Christian social ethics and the policy making of the Secular City than was asserted even in the Middle Ages. In the *contents* of ecumenical ethics there needs to be some way to tell some difference between the spiritual and the temporal power. Yet I fear that to propound this thesis even in an age that is assertedly post-Christian will only brand the author as one who believes the church to be a spiritual cult with no pertinent social outlook.

At least, those who affirm the church to be of necessity a sect in the world "come of age" should, to be consistent, call radically into question the identification of Christian social ethics with the enterprise of public policy formation. Their task should be the nurture of a Christian ethos within the autonomies of the modern world, and not by manifold thought and action to attenuate that ethos still more by eliding it into worldly wisdom. One cannot have it both ways, by declaring we have taken our exodus from "Christendom" while continuing to fashion Christian social ethics in the manner of the great cultural churches of the past. The oddity is that contemporary ecumenical social ethics evidences less acknowledgment of the separation between the church and the office of magistrate or citizen than was clearly acknowledged by the great cultural churches of the past—except perhaps by the claims made by the bull *Unum Sanctum* (Boniface VIII, November 18, 1302).

The *ad hoc* theology that today gives seeming warrant to this almost complete identification of Christian social ethics with social policy making is the view that the relevant contemporary knowledge of God and his claims upon us and the judgment and grace he enacts over humankind comes from "what God is doing in the world." Not only is

20

this evidently a fig leaf to cover the unseemly parts of a disintegrated Christian understanding. Not only is this an evident secularization of the church so that it may be brought into congruence with the autonomous decision making of men in the spheres in which they live in modern society. It is also the case that, since there can be a number of versions of what God is doing in the world, we must then go about faulting one another's consciences in the doing of particularistic ecumenical ethics.

To the biblical warrant adduced by appeal to the fact that the prophets were often quite specific in their judgments and in their advice to kings, it must simply be said that their example can hardly be cited by anyone who believes we are no longer even a religious people, and much less a political people of the Covenant. In any case, in most ages before the present one it was believed that, since the coming of Christ and in him the establishment of God's universal covenant with all mankind, there now are two cities, not one. The virtue and the price, so to speak, of this are that we must distinguish in the ecumenical city between ecumenical Christian ethics and the social, economic, and political policies of the peoples among whom we also dwell in historical pilgrimage.

I am aware of the fact that some of the things said forthrightly in this critique may simply be used as ammunition by those conservatives and right-wingers who on every occasion attack the NCC and WCC irrationally and indiscriminately. I am aware of this and would stop it if I could. But this is a risk that simply has to be accepted, if there is any hope of ever correcting the present polarization of so-called liberal religious opinion and so-called conservative religious opinion, which in substance look remarkably like the secular variety of the same opinions—plus, in each case, the little steam engine of religion that "thought he could."

21

The present writer aspires neither to the role of prophet nor to the role of Socratic gadfly. Still some things need to be said if no one else breaks silence. And it may be well to remember that if the gadfly is not welcomed and heard, then come the carrions and a corpse instead of the living body of Christ.

Before this volume is published, many events will have taken place both in the church and in the world about us. In either the life of the church or the political life of mankind it is difficult to step into the same river twice, since the stream of events will have moved on. This means that by the time this book is issued some of its material will already be somewhat dated.

In no significant respect will this alter the argument here set forth. It may be that historical events and events in the politics of Southeast Asia will have moved on (indeed, we prayerfully hope that they will have moved on) to the point where structures of peace can be established in Vietnam. It is, indeed, the task of statecraft so to act that solutions not now possible *become* possible in the future; and the statesmen of one nation are not the only actors engaged in doing this or responsible for thus shaping the future. This is the nature of the interactions that constitute diplomacy and the purposive use of armed force.

In any new constellation of political forces that historical events may bring forth, however, no Christian in the United States should then suppose that now at last his government has made peace—a "just endurable" peace—by peaceful means alone, while before we were doing wrong by fighting. Instead, the present arbitrament of arms—no less than, for example, somebody's mediation of the conflict—will both have served to make such an arrangement possible. At some future date it may be a live option for the powers that made by the Geneva Agreements in 1954 inadequate instruments for peace in Southeast Asia to be reconvened (Russia having finally agreed with Great Britain to reconvene it). But none of these eventualities would render these alternatives realistic options for a statesman's choice at the present time, or at the time the Conference on Church and Society met in the summer, 1966, and which some of the assembled churchmen may have had in mind in condemning recent United States policies and actions amid the present, still grim alternatives.

My criticism of the churches' syndrome of particular pronouncements will, therefore, undergo no essential change in the event that some specific proposal becomes a real possibility in the future. Indeed, it should be noticed that this criticism is not that such specific recommendations or incriminations are incorrect or that they could have been known in 1966 to be wrong or unrealistic, but that they were in any case too particular. The reader, therefore, need only read what follows with some historical perspective, if by that time it is a little dated in its details and illustrations.

There are also significant events in the life of the church that will be behind us by the time anyone reads these pages. The NCC Study Conference on Church and Society will meet in Detroit on October 22-26, 1967. These meetings will undoubtedly be an improvement over Geneva 1966 in that there will be fewer plenary addresses, more time for study and discussion, and better deliberations. But then the reader has only to remember that procedures for deliberation are not the only thing to be questioned. The question then will be: Were the aspired goals and the particularity of Church and Society unreformed at Detroit? These meetings will undoubtedly be more than a warming over of Geneva. They will focus attention upon the thought of Christians and the teachings of the churches in North America in the areas of poverty, race relations, and inter-

23

national affairs—with emphasis upon our responsibility in regard to world economic development. But then the question will be: In what fashion and for what good reasons or by what Christian warrants was the 1966 Geneva conference *presupposed* at Detroit? In any case, the argument of this book is that the Geneva Report cannot be made the basis or a basis for future discussion; and that we ought not any longer to proceed uninterruptedly weaving the texture of ecumenical Christian ethics by leapfrogging from pronouncement to pronouncement. The questions raised in this volume have to be fairly faced, and I do not believe they are going soon to be dated by events that are yet likely to be forthcoming in Church and Society. In this sense, it is altogether too easy to step into the same river twice—and to be inundated by the established practices.

One final prefatory remark. This little essay is sent forth seeking to be read not only, and perhaps not mainly, because I believe that I have laid hold of something that is correct and needs saying. It is not that, beyond subjective certitude, I am objectively certain that the current practices and goals of ecumenical ethics are wrong and in need of correction by my view of the truth. I need not even claim that I know that the methods and aspired goals of ecumenical ethics are partly true and partly false and therefore still in need of free, frank, and unlimited discussion that always seeks a fuller truth. These were only two of John Stuart Mill's apologies for freedom of expression and debate and for maximum conflict of opinion. The third reason he advanced for welcoming disagreement with any and all received opinions and practices was by far the more interesting one, and on this I want finally to rest my case.

"Let us assume," Mill wrote,[5] "that the received opinions and practices *are true*"; then we still need to "examine into the worth of the manner in which they are likely to be held when their truth is not freely and openly canvassed." The truth needs contention if it is to remain "living truth" and not "dead dogma" or routine practice. "This is not the way truth ought to be held by a rational being"—or, we may add, among the pilgrim people of God—since truth is not a quality "accidentally clinging" to words once enunciated, nor does worth thus cling to practices once established.

Something must be done to "keep up in the minds of believers a lively apprehension of the truth which they nominally recognize, so that it may penetrate the feelings and acquire a real mastery over the conduct." In the absence of discussion, too often not only the *grounds* of an opinion or habitual practice are forgotten but the *meaning* of the opinion or practice as well. "He who knows only his own side of the case knows little of that."

I judge that the able and hard-working members of what I call the social action curia would not in a cool hour disagree with this. At an hour past midnight at Geneva, Dr. Jon L. Regier, Associate General Secretary of Christian Life and Mission of the NCC, aptly described himself and his co-workers as "civil servants" of the churches. To them is due all proper praise—except a silence or a defense that does not agitate and enliven the manner in which the received practices and goals of the social ethics of the older ecumenical movement are likely to be held when their adequacy and truth are not freely and openly canvassed. In this way only are we likely to be ready for our destined meeting with the lively spirit of ecumenism that has arisen within Roman Catholicism.

Princeton University　　　　　　　　　Paul Ramsey
May 15, 1967

WHO SPEAKS
FOR THE CHURCH?

The Rev. Dr. W. A. Visser 't Hooft's farewell address as
General Secretary of the World Council of Churches [1] defended the right of church bodies to take a stand on controversial social and political issues. In defense of arriving
at "concrete conclusions," Visser 't Hooft rightly pointed
out that "concern for the victims of injustice and conflict
is a most spiritual matter"; and the church's province is
"spiritual matters."

From that point on, however, the retiring General Secretary's defense of specific policy recommendation by the
"church" to the "magistrate" raised more questions than it
answered.

For one thing, Visser 't Hooft pleaded that "we have
no right to give only counsels of perfection to statesmen and
other leaders who are faced with the ambiguities of politics
and have so often to choose between various courses, each
of which may have grave consequences." This supposed that
statesmen and other leaders are anxiously waiting for the
church to give them more from the storehouse of its political
wisdom. This will be news to them—especially when the
advice that is offered does not recognizably come from the
church's storehouse of political wisdom but likely arose from
a particular reading of the factors bearing on policy that
was already in public debate.

Faced as they are with "the ambiguities of politics" and beset in the public forum by counselors with equally accredited expertise crying "This way!" and "No, that way!" it is hard to imagine that many statesmen would feel their tasks made easier or their vision deepened by specific advice which yet seems to come from above the ambiguities. This advice is apt to have as grave consequences as any. No doubt political leaders need the strength and the correction that can only come from broad and sustained debate of political questions. But what if some part of this advice is believed to be specially authenticated because it comes from groups in our society that are supposed to be unusually sensitive to human need and can perhaps discern the *kairos* better? The magistrate is then apt to feel that many good people are crying "Peace! Peace!" in a world where there is no peace, and that we churchmen are simply not in the position to bear political responsibility for the consequences of the particular course proposed for choice if it should turn out to be disastrous.

However, the crucial objection to Visser 't Hooft's defense of the church's giving particular recommendations to statesmen should be directed against his assumption that the only alternative to this is that they be given "only counsels of perfection." Must those who undertake to speak for the church, or in the name of Christian truth, choose between abstract irrelevancies and policy-making exercises? The church has a proper role in addressing itself to the problems of political morality and the common life. We ought not to yield to those who say that the church should stay out of politics. That's as undifferentiated as the way too often we now get into politics. There needs to be a responsible and discriminating analysis of the church's proper address to political questions (and, secondarily, every effort should be made to improve the deliberative processes by which the

27

church and churchmen presume to speak). To this end, I propose a serious examination of the question, Must the churches choose between abstract, pious irrelevancies and policy-making exercises?

A first step toward breaking the hold that this disjunction has upon our social gospel minds can be taken by establishing once and for all that a congeries of policy recommendations, no matter how specific in each of its details, is as abstract a package, and as far from being possible national policy, as could be any general counsels of perfection. Along with this, the older half of the ecumenical movement needs to study seriously the example, the procedures and achievements of Vatican Council II (and of John XXIII) in speaking *relevantly* to social and political questions while avoiding even the appearance of unduly binding the conscience of the statesman in his decision because it was the church, or a group of churchmen, who spoke to him too much specific advice.

If we are to believe Visser 't Hooft's predictions, this will not be done. He promised that the conference on Church and Society convened by the World Council of Churches in Geneva, July 12-25, 1966, would try to reach concrete conclusions on the major social and international issues of the time. He said that these conclusions would exceed in specificity the somewhat general statements found in the "Pastoral Constitution on the Church in the Modern World" issued by the Second Vatican Council. Amid all today's critical situations having grave moral implications, he concluded that the churches have a duty "to become specific to the point of indicating in which direction the nation or nations should go." (Since on a fair reading the Vatican Council did that, Visser 't Hooft must have meant that the conference in Geneva should provide more specific directives than "direction.") The fact that the retiring General Secretary said no more than is already established in ecumenical practice does not make it right.

THE ABSTRACTNESS OF CONCRETE ADVICE

It can be shown that a series of specific policy proposals issuing from an assemblage of churchmen is, for all the particularity of each, as abstract as a counsel of perfection issuing from the same source, so far as the real requirements of the sound formation of an actual national policy are concerned. For the church to adopt the posture of giving concrete advice does not come any closer to shouldering the statesman's burden or illuminating his responsibilities for what must be done to hammer out the overall political policies of a nation (especially a nation that must have policies all over the world) than general directions to him concerning how he should shape events if he can. A series or a package of concretes is still a generality, I shall argue, until each is examined and corrected in the light of its effects on all other problems presently facing the nation anywhere in the world. No church council has ever assumed or ever can or should assume responsibility for this before it speaks to the world. Then the church had better not undertake the semblance of being concretely political in its utterances.

The opening words of a report on the proceedings and findings of the Sixth World Order Study Conference meet-

29

ing in St. Louis seem on first reading to be heavily laden with irony: "That 463 people from all sections of the nation could in a three-day meeting draw up and reach agreement on policy statements on all the major—and many of the minor—foreign policy issues affecting our country seems incredible. That, in addition, they listened attentively to eight addresses more or less pertinent to the subjects under discussion would tend to make this a minor miracle." [1] Those words were surely meant to call in question the worth of any such findings.

So it seems, until the correspondent's concluding remark that "the very fact that the delegates felt impelled to speak so forthrightly on a number of controversial issues is reassuring in a day when pressure to conform to Administration policy on foreign affairs is so strong." This seems to say that in this instance, because it was contrary-minded, a church assemblage did something that was indirectly good for the political society no matter what was the substance of its many specific resolutions. But this faint commendation was not left on that ground. The final verdict upon the St. Louis conference, we are told, depends on how "zealously" these "goals" are pursued by the NCC's International Affairs Commission and its participating communions!

In short, this conference represented only itself; it could not speak *for* the church or *for* the churches. It seemingly did very little to impose on itself by a self-denying ordinance the requirement that no more be said in addressing the urgent political problems of the present day than can clearly be said on the basis of Christian truth and insights. Yet the conference spoke very particularly *to* the churches and *to* the nation on a large number of very complex issues and problems. And now its findings are zealously to be made into precedental determinations of responsible Christian decisions and action in the political life of this nation.

An individual Christian (no matter what his political persuasion) may well feel that there is something fundamentally wrong in this kind of address to him.

At the moment, however, we are concerned to ask: Is this the way (without speaking for the church and without the self-limitation of saying only those "directions" that are clearly entailed in Christian truth and insights) to speak to the world, to magistrates, to the government?

Any assemblage can, of course, construct a number of historical predictions that have verisimilitude about the greater or lesser evil consequences that will come from the adoption of particular policies. There are always many such conjectures, supported by experts and by all sorts of facts, to which to succumb when representing only oneself. If these "pictures of the world" are opposed to those held in government circles, they can be used in adopting a pose of being prophetic in criticism of present policy and in support of some alternate policy. In this way it is easy to attain prophecy and at the same time a feeling of being deeply involved and relevant. Yet this yields maximalist church pronouncements that are both jurisdictionally beyond the "competence" of churchmen as such and also as distant as any general principle could be from actual policy making.

Thus does the church blur the distinction between itself and all other groups in the society which in any measure participate in the formation of public opinion; and it inordinately seeks to assume in the name of the church (which cannot be detached from these findings by any denials that this was meant) decisions that belong in the realm of the state. Unless it can be made clear in what way Christian teaching can as such substantively and compellingly lead to these conclusions, then this is simply to put the engine of religious fervor behind a particular partisan political point

31

of view which would have as much or as little to recommend it if it had not emanated from a church council.

The shrewdest device yet for accomplishing this purpose is the reservation that the resolutions and pronouncements on all sorts of subjects advising the statesman what he should do which issue from church councils (or from groups like the Clergy Concerned over Vietnam) in fact do not represent "the church" (or Christian morality) but only the views of the churchmen who happen to be assembled. Thus a group of concerned Christians free themselves from having to weigh their words lest they falsely commit the church and speak an inadequately Christian word to this age; and of course they are not in the position of the statesman who has to correct one policy by another and to bear the responsibility for any cost/benefits he may have left out of account. One can scarcely imagine a situation that to a greater extent invites irresponsible utterance, even while the participants feel they are being exceedingly responsible because they are talking in specifics and not in generalities. Precisely because, for historical and denominational reasons, councils convened by the NCC and the WCC cannot claim to speak *for* the church, there is even greater need for every effort to be made that they say only what can be said in the name of Christian truth in every utterance addressed to the church and to the world today.

The General Board of the NCC on December 3, 1965, did verbally refer its suggestions to the prudence of citizens and of statesmen and to the political process. "We, therefore, recommend," it said, "that the United States, in the interest of bringing peace and growing justice and freedom to the territories of Vietnam, should now consider the following suggestions." But from that point on followed a number of specifics such as "request the UN to begin negotiations," "request the UN, further, as soon as possible to convene a peace conference regarding Vietnam," "with representation from the National Liberation Front," without a shadow of a suggestion that nothing gives the General Board of the NCC the political wisdom to know whether this is an opportune moment or whether these are opportune things to do or not. At the same time, the injunctions that the bombing of North Vietnam cease for a sufficient period "with a simultaneous effort to induce the North Vietnam Government to stop sending military personnel and material into South Vietnam" shows that if you put together a couple of particulars you get a generality like "Let there be no war."

There were, of course, the necessary reservations about who was speaking. "Some believe. . . ." "Others believe. . . ." Then came a welcomed sentence: "We hold that within the spectrum of their concern Christians can and do espouse one or the other of these views and still other views and should not have their integrity of conscience faulted because they do." The first of these views was that of those Christians who "believe that the military effort should continue and that unless the spread of communism by violent infiltration is checked by further military means, liberties of not only South Vietnam but of Southeast Asia are imperiled. In this view the war must go on until the military results bring the Viet Cong and North Vietnamese to the conference table." It is hard to see how anyone holding that opinion, if it was represented on the board, could then have agreed with all of its particular policy statements. And certainly what was heard in the churches and by the world generally were these policy statements, and not that legitimate Christian position or the reservation that the NCC board does not speak for its member denominations or by its majority voice suppress points of view that are prominent in the churches.

33

Still, the church speaking would be improved if this NCC example in stating divergent Christian political premises or conclusions about national policy were followed by other groups as well. Other official and unofficial groups of Christians and journals of Christian opinion, in voicing their opinions and protests to the rest of the church and to the world, need to be equally candid in recognizing that there are equally valid contrary particular opinions held by other Christians who "should not have their integrity of conscience faulted because they do." Indeed, they need to have the same concern to include along with their own advice to statesmen such a clear statement of a contrary opinion.[2] This would keep it ever evident (to ourselves and to others), that there is no way to speak for the church, to be the church speaking relevantly to political questions, and at the same time to address particular prudential recommendations to the leaders of the nations. This would keep clear the fact that prudential political advice comes into the public forum with no special credentials because it issues from Christians or from Christian religious bodies. It would also prevent the (inadvertent or purposeful) putting together of a consensus on these political questions where there is and should be none. Something is radically wrong when churchmen in council have enormous reservations and problems over who is speaking ("Some say. . . ." "Others say. . . .") and yet few reservations about addressing specific political advice to a multitude of the world's problems. The careful reporting of divergent Christian positions is good if these are *general* points of view *relevant* to action, or Christian outlooks upon public policy. But if the reported disagreement was over the specifics of policy decision, and then a vote is taken, what goes out to the world is a particular statement that will have the same actual or aspired influence upon public policy as if it had been unanimous, and as if it had been asserted to be *the* Christian thing to do.

On the other hand, a bag of specifics is still a generality in relation to actual policy. For ecumenical councils on Church and Society responsibly to proffer specific advice would require that the church have the services of an entire state department. There would have to be officers permanently in charge of many, many separate "desks" whose responsibility would be to assess every proposed policy dealing with problems anywhere in the world and to urge the rejection or correction of these proposals in the light of repercussions upon the country or area each particular secretary should know more intimately than any other officer. And someone would have to resolve these interests, claims, and counterclaims into actual ventures of state. Otherwise, a recommendation like "Recognize China" or "Negotiate with the Viet Cong" is rather like the counsel "Do good" or "Feed the hungry."

This can be seen by what sometimes happens when wiser heads prevail in the general committees of the NCC or WCC than sometimes seize the floor in lesser councils. While holding on to many of the specifics, are these boards not often forced to a point above the ambiguities and above every actual political conflict? This is the meaning of statements calling down a plague upon both houses, and of recommendations that while the United States ought to do this, Hanoi ought to do that. Such statements wax irrelevant or erroneous while remaining specific when, for example, it is subtly suggested that the National Liberation Front is the political "parent" of the Viet Cong, when a statesman knows that (historically and actually) it is the political "arm" of the Viet Cong. These statements end by recommending that all sides be relentless in negotiation when—as our political leaders have to view the matter—the fact is that, e.g., the Viet Cong were through the summer of 1966 demanding settlement in accordance with the program of national liberation, i.e., no negotiation at all.[3] Thus, most of these balanced but apparently specific recommendations, brought to bear upon the realities in the midst of which the statesman lives and must decide and act, are actually rather to be compared to the counsel of perfection: "Make peace if you can." The magistrate cannot allow himself to believe (even if he sometimes yields to the ethos in saying so) that there is such a thing as "unconditional negotiations" on the part of a responsible power. The magistrate cannot allow himself to believe that disarmament can be achieved without first resolving some outstanding political conflicts. He should not naïvely suppose that the weaker the UN becomes as an apt decision-making, interventionary threat-removing, and interpositional peace-keeping body, the more the nations should load it with enormous problems they have not yet found to be corrigible to any of their own initiatives.

At the level of the Central Committee of the World Council of Churches it is evident that ecumenical statements, so long as they remain specific and are not wholly irresponsible, are forced to rise above the real situation in which political leaders must live and decide and act. Pieces of particular advice are still offered (this for the sake of feeling concretely involved in the world's problems), but these must be a balanced set of particulars (for the sake of being responsible, and not partisan). It is sun-clear that this manner of the church speaking puts together a package of specifics which amounts, when addressed to the statesman's actual world and his real options, to a counsel of perfection.

Thus the Central Committee of the WCC meeting in Geneva, February 16, 1966, adopted a resolution stating, among other things, (1) "that the United States and South Vietnam stop bombing of the North and North Vietnam stop military infiltration of the South" (this means there should be no war of subversion in Vietnam and no riposte to it needed); (2) that "arrangements be encouraged for negotiations between the Government of South Vietnam and the National Liberation Front in the hope that there may be found a negotiating authority representative of all South Vietnam" (this means there should be no civil war in South Vietnam; and if there were "a negotiating authority representative of all South Vietnam" none would be needed); (3) "that in order to relieve present international tension the United States review and modify its policy of 'containment' of Communism, and Communist countries supporting 'wars of liberation' review and modify their policy" (this means, Let there be peace).

No wonder John Cogley commented in his report of this NCC resolution in *The New York Times,* February 17, 1966, that to say these things is "to demand that both sides agree to put an end to the war, a sentiment appropriate for a church body but hardly of such political significance as to involve the churchmen in controversy." With such leadership, it is no wonder that a great many people today imagine they have *said* something and *done* something responsible when they march with banners reading "Make Love, not War."

This is enough to show that balanced pairs of pieces of specific advice are no more than pious and irrelevant generalities issuing from a great distance above the problems facing the nations.

There is, however, a way, and (so far as I can see) only one way, to avoid this, while as *churchmen* still making particular political judgments. (This second way of remaining specific I in no sense endorse.) That would be to condemn forthrightly some concrete current practice or policy and then place beside this only a recommendation that statesmen search for an option on the optimistic premise that if present policy is so certainly censurable there must be an alternative that is presently practicable.

On one reading, this was the device used at the Geneva Conference in July, 1966, when one of the reports specifically condemned nuclear war in such an unqualified way that no conceivable use of any nuclears in any war (and consequently no deterrence of nuclear war) would be either possible or morally permissible for one moment after the unlikely event that the statesmen of the great powers took seriously this instruction.[4] Then, among other things, this same report hedged the "realism" of its undiscriminating condemnation by calling for greater "imagination" on the part of "all the established powers" in this world. It condemned "lack of confidence" for bedeviling "the relations between the states of Europe," and addressed itself to the "real" problem of "how the supreme task, to avoid nuclear war, can be carried out" by listing among the "measures" that "would help" a recommendation that the "mere balance of power" be changed "into a community with institutions for the prevention of escalation of conflict between the main powers."[5] Obviously this measure is the same as the aspired goal and thus can help not at all in getting there. This is a direction of action, not a specific directive; and it is certainly a direction which churches and churchmen are competent to chart. But to condemn specifically and sweepingly while recommending alternatives in properly general terms is surely the way to succeed as prophets without really trying.

I want to give two additional illustrations of this procedure of placing beside a condemnation of some particular policy not a balancing condemnation that is equally particular, but only a plea that there must be some other way. One is the telegram sent to President Johnson by Visser 't Hooft and O. Frederick Nolde, the director of the Commission of the Churches on International Affairs, on July 1, 1966. The other is the editorial in *Christianity and Crisis*, "We Protest the National Policy in Vietnam," March 7, 1966. These will show that particular political protests need not be forced to a distance above the actual problem (as in the case of well-balanced censures of both sides). Instead, when we stick with the ambiguities of politics and the undiminished crunch of political forces, our protests are required to take the form of rather excruciating assertions that present policy is wrong and pleas to the side in conflict that is most likely to be susceptible to moral exhortation. The balance between specific recommendations to both sides is undone; one alone is held firm without acknowledging that the practicability of this depended on simultaneous acceptance of the other also. The specific policy condemned or recommended is then coupled no longer with actions in the real political world that condition its practicability, but with pleas to be more imaginative or to venture more in milking from the ambiguities the always less grim alternatives that must somehow be there.

Thus the telegram sent to President Johnson reached back to establish a connection with the policy statement of the Central Committee on February 16, 1966; but it mentioned only its warning against intensified bombing and dropped out any repetition to its recommendation that North Vietnam stop military infiltration of the South. It spoke, of course, of the costs both sides are paying and exacting. The telegram was, as we shall see, far more responsible than the Geneva Conference in letting this pair of particular recommendations become unstuck, and more accurate concerning events since February, 1966, when it stated:

39

"We appreciate that the United States has offered to stop bombing North Vietnam on condition that North Vietnam cease infiltration of the South and deeply regret that no affirmative response has been forthcoming." Nevertheless, these church leaders wanted the United States to stop the bombing anyway. *On what grounds?* "Fidelity to its own tradition," "by virtue of its position as a dominant power in the world today," "bitter racial and other resentments against the U.S.A. and the West," the suffering of the Vietnamese people, and the danger of escalation. *What measures should the United States take?* It should "intensify its effort to move without delay from the battlefield to the conference table," "explore every means both pragmatic and imaginative towards this end," by "recourse" to the United Nations, initiatives by its Secretary General, or by reconvening the 1954 Geneva Conference—and, of course, prayer to almighty God. The telegram did not note that these things are ways to try to bring the bombing to an end along with ending the infiltration. It spoke as if renewed trials of these things could simply be coupled with stopping the action of one side. Thus a prophetic protest against the United States intensification of aerial bombing in early summer, 1966, and the seeming realism of stopping it, was hedged by appeals to "alternatives" that have been tried and are constantly under review by the United States government. There are some people who believe that it is important for WCC Study Conferences and its Central Committee to come up with specific policy recommendations in order for the church to be able to speak promptly through telegrams such as this sent forth between meetings of ecumenical conferences or of the WCC Central Committee!

The statement of editorial policy in *Christianity and Crisis,* March 7, 1966, also condemned in a very specific fashion without taking responsibility for the alternatives, or even for the conviction that there are any. It petered out into a comparison of "various possibilities with the present grim realities," without (of necessity) a sufficient penetration of any of these possibilities to see if they might not be grimmer. The editorial board's statement warranted this technique of censuring the real in the light of several ideals by the excuse that we should not look for "painless ways" out. The political question, however, is whether there is a way out, not a painless one; and any out that is less painful in facing all the grim realities. A statesman has to determine *this;* groups of Christians when speaking as such do not. It remains, however, open to them to condemn the present policy as worse than a number of possibilities not yet tested by reality, and to urge our statesmen to use their "moral imagination."

Here we come upon the generality that sustained in this protest its seeming realism and the seeming responsibility of its specific advice. It is easy to wax prophetic as long as one deals only in hypotheticals. A statesman, however, has to be beforehanded while, amid the grim realities and the actions that come upon him, he posits a single course of action whose consequences he must take responsibility for saying will be less grim.

It required only twenty-four hours after taking the Vietnam conflict to the UN to display the fact that an opportune moment for this had not yet arrived. Yet proponents of this proposal, so long as it was only an untried specific possibility, could easily gain accolades for greater idealism or greater realism over our political leaders who on four separate occasions thought this through and judged it unrealistic.[6] There ought to be better ways for churchmen to be the church speaking to the magistrate, and for them to help sustain the ethos out of which statesmanship may come.

This leads in the direction away from specific utterances.

Was it in the other direction of constituting a "shadow" state department that Visser 't Hooft pointed when he acknowledged that the churches were not fully prepared for the new role many of them are assuming of giving specific recommendations to political leaders? To a greater use of churchmen who are political experts? To a better "methodology" for determining which specifics should specifically be said?

Was it in this same direction that the Geneva Conference on Church and Society pointed, when it stated that "real dialogue is needed" and that in the churches "an example of true community transcending the nations must be manifested"?[7] Does the older ecumenical movement hope to transcend the peoples among whom Christians are mingled in this world, not in the direction of clearer statement of Christian action-relevant perspectives upon the world's problems but in the direction of a universal view of concrete political policies for the world's statesmen? The latter seemed to be envisioned by the statement that to "make critical social and ethical judgments in a Christian perspective, the first essential is knowledge of the facts."[8] The worth of knowing the facts, of course, cannot be denied; but how are these fact-filled concrete universal judgments upon all the world's problems to be arrived at? The call seemed to be for the church to transcend the peoples of the world in the direction of a universal political community and not in the direction of some better form of universal ecclesiastical community in which churchmen exchange views and speak *ad extra* only on the basis of the Christian insights they should be exploring and deepening. The call was for "an exchange between nations of delegations of people for the purpose of conversation and dialogue on matters of war and peace as an expression of love and our interdependent relationship"; [9] and later we will see how specific was the American delegation's reason for wanting such exchanges: to help bring about a revision of this nation's Vietnam policy.

No one can question the need for many new means of ecumenical dialogue, if this has in view the deepening and broadening of ecumenical Christian political ethics. The Geneva Conference, however, had in view that such periodic consultations would keep developing situations "under constant review" and propose "suitable collective action." [10] The main body of this report recommended that the WCC be responsible for "the collection, critical evaluation, and dissemination of relevant facts to all the constituent churches" and that "the constituent churches should for their part collect clear information on situations of ecumencial importance for passing on to the appropriate department of the WCC." [11] Was this to the end that the ecumenical city increase its fact-filled competence in specific policy making? That would be a move in the direction of constituting at the world level a "shadow" state department believed to be competent to deal with the specific issues of international politics and economics.

This would be the reverse of the most urgent need at this hour. Certainly, the procedures of church councils sponsored by the older half of the modern ecumenical movement need to be radically improved so that sounder deliberations can be insured. But the aim of these procedures and deliberations should not be to improve the church's speaking to the world its supposedly expert specific advice, but to make sure that in everything addressed to the churches and to the world today our church councils can better speak *for* the church, for the whole of Christian truth, and every saving word but no more than can be said upon this basis. Even if these councils do not officially represent their participating denominations, we need to know that so far as humanly possible in their deliberations and pronouncements they nevertheless are in a real sense trying to be the church speaking.

We now have before us three possibilities, each in one way or another demonstrating how abstract can be the specific advice of the church or from Christians as such to the world: (1) a well-balanced set of specific condemnations, rising above the ambiguities, "judging" both sides in some historic conflict or arbitrament of arms; (2) specific condemnation of one side only or mainly, coupled with the recommendation that political leadership imaginatively or creatively search for solutions that must be possible and are bound to be less grim than the present course of action; and (3) a possible final corruption of the social teachings of world Christianity if, on account of our captivity to the notion that the church's address to the world must be in terms of specific recommendations and condemnations, we should yield to the dream of becoming a surrogate world political community, each where we are and in our various groupings particularly instructing one another and then telling the governments of the world how to bring about the solutions, the peace that passeth understanding.

This is enough to set anyone off in search of a way between irrelevant generalities and specific pronouncements.

None of the foregoing is intended to deny the importance of the transnational Christian community, which is more and more realized and realizable today, and which has always been a principal goal of the ecumenical movement. Nor should anyone deny that the worldwide Christian community can be of very real indirect aid to statesmen in the nation-state system. The unknown easily becomes the enemy, and channels of communication which are maintained despite national differences, even in wartime, have many political uses and general benefits. Indeed, variations (1) and (2) above—striking out the too particular recommendations or incriminations—would look remarkably like what I call direction giving. But the foregoing is intended to deny that the world church or ecumenical ethics should pour itself into the mold of particular policy formation. That mold needs to be broken.

BETWEEN GENERALITY
AND PARTICULARITY

We have to distinguish between the "direction" of action and a "directive" for the action, between decision-oriented or action-related economic, social, and political analysis following from Christian themes, and specific policy formation that cannot be elaborated on this basis. These have to be distinguished even if there is not an entire separation to be made, and even if the distinction itself is only relative. Our aim should be to discover the narrow or broad ridge between generalities and particularities, and to tell whether anything Christian and anything important can be said along this way. This, and this alone, can make the case for ecumenical ethics, or for their being a Christian social ethics.

I shall not myself undertake to determine exactly where the line should be drawn, or any complete characterization of a Christian direction of action in contrast to policy

45

directives. It is enough for a "Critique of Ecumenical Reasoning" to have demonstrated that there are these limits, and to point out the contradictions of one another's "prudences" into which we fall when the limits are violated in quest of excessive particularity in judgments concerning the noumenal—the ambiguous—world of politics.

There must be this distinction, there must be this third alternative between generality and particularity, unless we are to say that the fact of twilight abolishes the distinction between day and night. We had better not argue from the twilight—from the relative concreteness of decision-oriented directions—to the conclusion that we cannot tell when darkness comes and we have entered the obscurities of specific prudential decisions where the directives any other man or any other Christian points us to cannot be faulted. These cannot be faulted by anything we have drawn from the light of day, or from the shadows thrown upon our twilight by the light of Christ.

It would be better to assume that we know the twilight from our knowledge of day and night. It would be better to assume that we may remain uncertain about whether we have rightly determined the directions for action that Christians should be addressing to the world of today precisely because we *do* know the difference between the ultimates of the Christian faith not yet prolonged into life and made ready for action, on the one hand, and, on the other, specific recommendations which may or may not prove to be (as their proponents believe, and disagree in believing) a proper fulfillment or application of these Christian directions for action.

The reason, therefore, why I shall not attempt to draw the line exactly or undertake a complete determination of the nature and meaning of a direction for action in contrast to a directive for policy is because this should be our common task, and it is the work of no one person alone, in the doing of ecumenical ethics. Once our passion for conscience-faulting and conscience-easing and public pressure-forming particulars is curtailed, none of us knows the contours or the content of the ecumenical ethics of the future. Nor will we ever know if anything else or anything less is taken as our common aim than a return to the fundamentals of Christian social ethics; and to the task of elaborating in this light and in the shadows cast by this light over the historical life of mankind whatever may be the decision-oriented and social action-relevant perspectives upon policy decisions that may be forthcoming.

This may be the place, however, for me to grasp the nettle of a seemingly telling objection posed to me by two persons who did me the courtesy of reading the manuscript of this volume, and who (I take it) are in different degrees not wholly unsympathetic with a number of my theses. Professor Ralph Potter, of Harvard Divinity School, writes: "I take it that at some point, perhaps at the gateway of Auschwitz, the Christian should speak very specifically against the outrageous crimes of his government. How does he decide when that time has come?" And Professor Thomas Derr of Smith College, the author of a chapter on "The Development of Modern Ecumenical Political Thought" for one of the Geneva preparatory volumes,[1] writes:

There must be a limit to the giving of directions which leave open the particular actions to be performed by the statesmen [and leave open the particular decisions of citizens]. Doesn't there come a point when the church simply has to say *no* to a particular policy (e.g. the church in Nazi Germany), and doesn't this *no* also frequently imply a particular *yes,* a specific alternative policy? As I think about what you propose as models of church speech in the political realm, I wonder if the reform needed isn't simply a deeper sense of the ambiguities of political life, a sense that might modify the tone of church statements, but which still has to contain the possibility of specific utterance and directives on *some* issues. The rub is how to decide *which* issues.

It is obvious, however, that the church's No to a particular policy, however justified upon clear Christian warrants, does not "frequently imply a particular *yes*." It implies this only when the alternatives are reduced to one only, i.e., only when there is but one specific policy for a nation that, for example, is contrary to Auschwitz. This, surely, is hardly ever the case; and indeed the opposites of Auschwitz are statable in terms of political principles or of structures and due processes for the domestic political society of a nation—which then require that Christians advance their reasons for these things and nurture them in the ethos of the church and in the ethos of the nation, no less than their warrants for saying a particular No in the emergency situation of outrageous crimes.

Still I do have to reply to the objection that, since this particular No is required of us, the weight I give to directions for policy emanating from churchmen meeting as such, in contrast to particular directives, is shown by this example to be misplaced.

The first thing to be said is that this case is an exception. It is an exception that proves the rule to which it is an exception. This was clearly an exception that proved itself in the clarity that required the Confessional Church in Germany to confess its faith and life before God by this particular No to outrageous crimes. This case, however, cannot be an open sluice gate through which pours the justification of all sorts of other particular Noes and Yeses concerning the policies to be adopted in the various sectors of society. Each would need to have the same clear warrant in Christian faith and morals attributable to this one. Only rarely do churchmen *as such* like Karl Barth and Reinhold Niebuhr have the "competence" to call, in the name of Christian responsibility, for a specific military resistance at its price—or for a particular peace at its price. The counting of these costs/benefits is ordinarily the work of political prudence which we Christians with all men exercise as the citizens and "lesser magistrates" of our several nations.

Two things happen when appeal is made to Christian responsibility for resistance to Hitler's outrageous crimes and for taking up arms against the terribly evil Nazi regime to prove that the churches should ordinarily seek to engage in particular policy decisions, recommendations, and incriminations. First, we find ourself counting the *benefits* of a particular peace or a particular de-escalation or of a particular way to try to introduce reconciliation into the field of political forces, and do not with equal realism count also the possible *costs* of each of these things. This is not the way statecraft must view the options. Second, and more important, since few such specific recommendations or negations are a matter of the church's need to confess its faith and life under the lordship of Christ, we find ourselves saying Yes or No beyond the Christian warrants on all sorts of subjects on which there may properly be legitimate, conscientious disagreement. We recommend specific policies knowing full well that another particular policy cannot on discernible Christian principle be altogether excluded from possible endorsement by another Christian who belongs with us in the same confessing church and who testifies with his life (maybe even in this contrary prudential judgment of his) to the same Christ. The danger, therefore, is that in our official and semiofficial church conferences we may let ourselves speak

49

to the world in behalf of partisan political proposals (which may, indeed, be wise—for all we know). The peril that stands close to the elbow is that we turn the church inside out and render it entirely congruent with secular decision making, abolishing all distinction between the temporal and the spiritual power in the content of ecumenical ethics. Thus we would identify "the church speaking" with the engine of religion put behind particular Yeses and Noes that have other ground (perhaps, indeed, sufficient ground) in worldly wisdom. Since this was not done expressly on the premise that the churches, like any other institution in our society, should contribute to the "continuing education" of its constituents but in the name of Christian teachings, this pattern of particular proclamation cannot fail to be accompanied by the ineluctable attentuation of the substance of Christian understanding in our churches and its weakening in the culture generally.

The second thing to be said in reply to this objection is that it is much too late if the church and Christians speaking as such have nothing to say until men stand at the gateway of Auschwitz, or if they have nothing or little to say concerning the commonweal before marauding bands of Nazis begin to engage in "direct action" in politics by violation of the commandment "Thou shalt not kill." Even such judgments are, of course, to be praised because they say more than that the church should be let alone to preach the Word and administer the sacraments. These were cries against outrageous crimes in the public order. A No was uttered before the church itself was touched. Still it is obvious that for this confession of the faith and life of the church to be wrung from it at this late hour (or only because the sixth commandment had been violated) had importance only for the present and future life of the church and perhaps for future actions of state. Such belated specific condemnation in the emergency situation of outrageous crimes can hardly be taken as a model of the church speaking to the world!

Yet appeal is made today to this case of the church's specific witness at the gateway to martyrdom not only to generalize to a program of Yeses and Noes as the proper form of the church's address to public questions, but also to mount an attack upon the sort of shaping, discriminating, and nourishing address to the environing culture which if effectively "spoken" long, long before the gateway to Auschwitz might have been of some real help to the earthly commonweal.

It continues to be sweepingly asserted that the doctrine of "orders of creation" or the idea that God's will can in some measure be known immanently from the meaning of "natural justice" was at fault; that this led in logic to the notion that *der Führer* was the manifestation of this will concretely. The truth is that the "German Christians" abused the notion that in part God's will may be immanent within his creation. To correct that "abuse" the Confessing Church rightly appealed to the sovereignty of God over the entire creation, to the sixth commandment revealed from above, and to the lordship of Christ. However, no one should forget the countervailing historical "abuse" to be found in the pre–Barmen Declaration posture of the divine right kings: Theirs was an abuse of the notion that God's will is wholly extrinsic to political processes and comes from above to impose righteousness upon the world. To correct this abuse, Calvinists of the left wing not only appealed to a sovereignty far higher than the divinity that hedged the king. Their confession of the faith and life of the church appealed also to an immanent justice in support of wars of civil and religious liberty.

Continued reliance (by a horrendous *ad hominem*) on the case of the church's specific condemnation at the gateway to Auschwitz is exceedingly apt to stop us from deep and extensive exploration of all the ethico-political insights that need to be articulated in the public forum long before Auschwitz and for which church thought and Christian social ethics have some competence. For it is not only the "prolongation" of natural justice in the direction of action for as far (and only as far) as this will take us that is eschewed. It is also the "prolongation" of any of the ultimate principles of Christian ethics—revealed ethics—for as far (and only as far) as this will take us that is omitted, in our passion for pronouncing too particularly upon urgent public questions.

The foregoing may seem an elaborate way of saying a very simple thing, namely, that for Christians to say No to outrageous crimes is one thing, while for them to say Yes or No to the recognition of Red China (for example) or her admission to the United Nations is quite another thing. The latter specific political action is susceptible to alternative moral or political characterization, and proposals or moves in regard to mainland China are matters on which there can be honest disagreement without contradicting any fundamental Christian moral principle or insight into politics. Genocide is not the same kind of thing as the relative answers that may be given to the question how to act responsibly to the end that Red China be no longer isolated and self-isolated from the rest of the world. The one is a fit subject of church pronouncements; the other is not.

There are, however, more decision-oriented directions for action than the sun gives when it rises in the morning. There are structures governing the good political community that Christians have an understanding of. These we have to think out, in the direction of the ambiguities, all the way up to the point where there arises legitimate disagreement as to the practice required by these Christian and general moral warrants. Explicit theological and moral criteria or tests are to be employed at every stage of our discussions and in every instance of official or semiofficial church promulgation. There must not be a careless and confused amalgam of theological, moral, and technical judgments, but rather a clear sorting out of the questions and issues in theological and ethical terms. However great the overlap in particular instances, there are nonetheless vital distinctions to be made between Christian moral judgments on the one hand and particular political, legal, and military judgments on the other; or between what is morally permitted or prohibited and what is tactically or prudentially advisable and practicable. The pronouncements of churchmen, meeting as such, ought to be limited to the former realm. Then if and when we speak on particular matters these should be clearly incapable of alternative moral characterization.

The Methodist General Conference rightly charted a direction for action when it declared that "every phase of a nation's foreign policy must be judged in part by whether it makes possible disarmament under law." Pope John XXIII in *Pacem in terris* stated the right course when he wrote that "the public authorities of the individual political communities . . . no matter how much they multiply their meetings and sharpen their wits in efforts to draw up new juridical instruments, . . . are no longer capable of facing the task of finding an adequate solution to present world problems"—"because of a *structural defect* [in the international system] which hinders them." The strength of the Geneva report lies in the fact that it, too, charted this same direction (and other directions) for action.

But beyond this there remain a good many policy decisions concerning how best to achieve "disarmament under law" and to correct the "structural defect" of the nation-state system, which Christians as such should not try to foreclose in the slightest degree. It was arguable, for example, that the Multilateral Nuclear Force would strengthen "Europe" politically, and that the achievement of this regional political unity would in the long run contribute to the larger unity of mankind. The contrary, of course, was arguable too. By the same token, a Christian can in good conscience believe that national initiatives, even initiatives leading to the use of force by a responsible power, cannot be excluded. Indeed, it can be argued that it is possible for a statesman to serve the international legal order directly but not well, by permitting an erosion of the power environment which will contribute ultimately to greater weakness in the international system we are struggling to develop[2] and to which the churches have pointed. Specific decisions upon these questions are the work of political prudence shaping the future by its particular decrees.

There are in all these and many other matters a number of moral choices that may sincerely be accepted even by persons who view political questions in the light of the same Christian ethical perspectives. For us to pronounce upon them in our conferences would be to try to lead decision one way, and beyond any good reason or Christian warrant for doing so.

Attempts to influence decision lead us away from clarifying the twilight by the light of Christ and by analysis of the shadow he casts over human historical and political existence, and away also from the meaning of natural justice, of the *esse* and *bene esse* of politics, that might have been drawn forth from Christian understanding. Instead, by concentrating on particular conclusions that can be reached, and by intervening with these in the discussion of a Christian's citizenship and the decisions that must be reached in the various sectors of society, we turn the church inside out. Christian address to the world becomes identified with a number of specific partisan positions that may or may not be correct. The church becomes a *secular* "sect" in its ecumenical ethics set over against the world as it is, instead of becoming truly a Christian sect concerned to nurture a distinctive ethos set over against an acculturated Christianity or against a culture that is no longer Christendom. This is surely a form of culture-Christianity, even if it is not that of the great cultural churches of the past. This is, indeed, the most barefaced secular sectarianism and but a new form of culture-Christianity. It would identify Christianity with the cultural vitalities, with the movement of history, with where the action is, with the next and even now the real establishment, but not with the present hollow forms. By contrast, true prophesy to the most high God would be impelled in this or any other age to speak words of judgment to precisely the existing cultural vitalities—against both Baalism and the Baalization of Yahwehism!

There is, in addition, a realistic and yet a consoling word that Christians should never fail to speak to magistrates and citizens and the people of the whole world, namely, that the world in which we live and all its urgent problems is an objectification of all our Babylonian hearts.[3] The finely woven texture of specific ecumenical pronouncements seems to add up to the prospect that this can or will cease to be the state of affairs with which we are dealing. Thus the shadows in the twilight cast by the enactment of God's judgment over our fallen existence cease—proposal by proposal—to be an operative part of the apt directions we bring to bear upon social problems; and the church's outlook becomes identified with that strange, current optimism about the autonomies of decision making in the secular city. This too is another form of culture-Christianity.

Moreover, this identification of Christian social ethics

with specific partisan proposals that clearly are not the only ones that may be characterized as Christian and as morally acceptable comes close to the original and the New Testament meaning of *heresy*. It introduces divisions into the life that may properly be a confession of the faith of the church. This, at least, was Paul's meaning when he condemned the factions (*hairesis*) among the Corinthians (I Cor. 11:18, 19), and when he enjoined the Christians in Rome, "Do not let what is good to you be spoken of as evil" (Rom. 14:16) : "For why should my liberty be determined by another man's scruples?" (I Cor. 10:29).

One practical way to avoid introducing factions into the life that may be our witness to the church and to the world would be for those of us who go to Church and Society conferences to take along with us in our minds a "counterpart"—a fellow Christian we know who disagrees with us on specific economic, social, and political conclusions, whose particular "scruples" are different from ours, but who (we cannot deny) thinks about his life and his responsibilities upon the same basis that we do. We should, of course, wrestle with that man for the particular verdict on all these questions, in hours past midnight when we have opportunity to discuss these questions together, or in journals of Christian opinion whose columns are open to a diversity of views on public questions and that have not settled down to some predictable liberal or conservative consensus. But with such a counterpart brought along with us, we could scarcely pronounce against him, not even in conferences speaking only for themselves. The latter excuse is long past credibility. It is doubtful whether this reservation was ever meant to lessen the effect or the authority of the conclusions reached, and it certainly cannot be denied that such verdicts are received, both by our fellow churchmen and by the world, as the church speaking (or trying to). To take such a counterpart along with us would enliven the self-denying ordinance that we need to impose on ourselves when we gather and presume to speak as churchmen. Then we might not so often call evil what we well know may be good in the particular conscientious judgments of others with whom we should not break faith or break the life—the one body of Christ.

THE CHURCH AND
SOCIETY SYNDROME:
THE GENEVA CONFERENCE

It is time now to give a rather full account of selected aspects of the Geneva Conference on Church and Society and of its findings. In attempting this I shall speak first of the procedures by which this conference conducted its deliberations and reached its findings and conclusions; and in this connection we will bring into view the manner in which Christian theological issues in social ethics were brought to bear (or failed to be brought to bear) upon the topics discussed at Geneva. Second, I propose to take up one of the most controversial conclusions of this conference, its specific condemnation of recent United States actions in Vietnam. Third, I shall attempt to throw some light on the question how much genuine dialogue there was between Christians who have the responsibilities of citizens of one of the great powers and Christians whose lot is cast with the peoples of smaller and developing countries, by examining some of the actions taken as individuals and as groups by persons from the United States present at the conference. Fourth, I offer an analysis of the Geneva statement on nuclear war, and of the plenary addresses at the conference on peace in the nuclear age.

This will be followed by an attempt to formulate in a

provisional model how the pronouncements of churchmen might be more responsibly expressed if they are going to continue to deal in specifics. Then we will be ready to ask, in the penultimate section of this volume, what may be learned from the newer (Roman Catholic) ecumenical movement about the church's proper address to society and to urgent modern problems, and from the deeper study of the issues of Christian faith and life now being undertaken by "Faith and Order."

1. In speaking of the deliberative procedures at the conference, of the *prima facie* lack of adequate deliberation sufficient to sustain its numerous findings, I shall not go back of the conference itself. I shall not go into the question concerning how precisely these participants and not quite another group of participants (numerically the same from the various countries, and in the same proportion of lay to clergy, or in the various professions, etc.) were assembled; or what this may or may not indicate concerning possible bias already advertently or inadvertently built into the conclusions of the conference before anyone actually arrived in Geneva, or what this says concerning the authority or expertness anyone should attribute to its findings. On the books, the conclusions were only the conclusions of the conference itself; and the important question to ask is whether this very interesting and capable group of participants was given or could have been given the procedures that would have enabled it to reach responsibly the conclusions it did.

In passing, however, two things may be noted. The first is that while there were more laymen than clergymen, a good proportion of the laymen were academics, and these were lumped together as "clerical" by the businessmen and other "practical" decision makers who were present. Second, the most notable gap in "representation," if this was to have been a predominantly lay conference competent to pronounce on international affairs, was the absence of Christian laymen who share responsibility at the middle echelon of government for decisions made in the executive departments, in state and defense departments, for example. The people from government were more often from the legislative branch. Yet in recent decades under the pressure of urgent modern problems and in agreement with the urgings of former councils of churchmen saying we need "a responsible society," there has taken place a vast expansion of the initiative of the administrative branches of government in determining public policy. Are there not a great number of Christian laymen now doing this who might have a good deal to contribute to the churches in our continued speech about responsible government? This lack at Geneva was in part made up for by two or three outstanding Dutchmen who have for more than a decade been engaged in manifold efforts of thought and administrative as well as legislative action to bring the European community into existence. It is notable that a frequent description of these men voiced by members of the American delegation was that they were more pro-American than the Americans! This characterization was correct, but the substantive meaning to be given to it is that such men were able to speak for Christian responsibility in the structures of government in a way few Americans were by vocation prepared to do.[1]

The point to be made concerning the conference itself has to do with its structures, its procedures; whether these were responsible ones; and, indeed, whether with the best will and intelligence in the world on the part of the participants, the deliberation made possible by the conference procedures could responsibly reach the conclusions it is said the conference reached. We have been calling for decades for responsible society, responsible government. It is high time for this judgment to be turned on ourselves. We should be resolved to say no more about responsibility in society until we have done something about responsible deliberation, and the procedures necessary for this to be made possible, at conferences sponsored by the churches, the NCC and the WCC. I at least would not be able to sleep nights if I thought that decisions of my government concerning problems of middle-range importance and urgency were resolved as rapidly and carelessly and *necessarily* with as little debate as the Geneva Conference presumed to reach particular conclusions of earthshaking importance —which with unnoticed irony often implied irresponsibility on the part of one or another government.

That 410 people from all over the world could in two weeks draw up approximately 118 paragraphs of "conclusions" concerning church, society, government, and "Christians in the Technical and Social Revolutions of Our Time" (which number of findings of fact and of value can probably be trebled, since many of the numbered conclusions to the four section reports are themselves made up of from three to five or six conclusions, each on very complex and troubling questions), seems incredible. That, in addition, they listened to two dozen conference plenary addresses of varying lengths and more or less pertinent to the subjects under discussion would tend to make this a major miracle. The only thing more incredible would be for someone now to affirm that the final verdict upon the Geneva Conference depends on how zealously these goals and prescriptions are pursued by the WCC and its participating communions and by the Commission of the Churches on International Affairs.[2] This is precisely the result many of the participants, and not least of all many of the Americans, went to Geneva to secure. These persons were already persuaded that leverage had to be got upon the topmost voices in the ecumenical movement who are not unnaturally concerned (if somewhat minimally, because of the long established Church and Society syndrome) still to speak *for* the whole church and not just *to* it in a predetermined way, or from some politically sectarian viewpoint.

This was supposed to be a "study" conference. It was even said in one of the documents concerning the intent and the procedures of the conference that "this is a thinking conference and not a legislative conference. We must avoid giving the impression that we have come to offer final answers or resolutions to the churches. We are weighing outlooks and pointing to issues." That was an auspicious beginning; but, as it turned out, there was no more than a semantic distinction to be drawn between reports transmitted to the churches for further study and "resolutions to the churches" or "conclusions" of the conference. Yet of the latter there were many. Anticipating this, the parliamentary procedures governing debate and voting in the final plenary sessions were distributed at the start; these procedures, for a study conference, were a revision of the procedures at the last WCC *policy* conference at New Delhi.

What meaning were the "conclusions" of the conference supposed to have, and what use was to be made of them? The planning committee met two days before the conference opened, and on the following day this was enlarged by the presence of the chairmen, rapporteurs, co-opted staff, etc., of each of the sections and subsections. To this larger group was presented a piece of procedural wisdom committed by some typist or mimeograph machine that, one cannot but think, would have been far superior to what the planning committee meant to use in directing the study conference. The motion for presenting the reports of the sections for debate in conference plenary read as follows: "That this report be received for inclusion in the general conference report;

and that its conclusions be adopted for transmission to the World Council of Churches and its member churches for their study, consideration and appropriate action." If this had been the order of the day, the two-week meeting in Geneva would have been but the beginning of a long continuing study of the church in a revolutionary age; and, what is more important, the time spent in Geneva could have been devoted entirely to confronting the many issues on the agenda and to genuine dialogue that might have gone deeper had we not been placed under the necessity of reaching a set of conclusions.

But, of course, this is not the way "Church and Society" is accustomed to proceed. John Bennett objected that it had been agreed in planning committee that the conference could "issue statements in its own name." It was promptly agreed that the motion should read: "That its conclusions be adopted by the conference and transmitted to the WCC, etc., for their study, etc." Thus, each section was expected to produce both a "report" to be only "received," and also "conclusions" to be "adopted." This, of course, was a proper correction of the typist's error, else there would have been no point to the press coverage that had been arranged for the final plenary sessions. The conference *had* to speak to the world its definitive conclusions on all sorts of subjects, following the most extraordinarily limited deliberations, I imagine, that have ever been directed by an ostensibly responsible and individually capable group of people to so many vast, urgent, and controversial questions.

No one came with "position papers" or preliminary drafts of the report. This, of course, was the way to encourage full discussion, especially on the part of laymen and people from churches in the developing or undeveloped countries who were present at this conference in greater numbers than

63

ever before and who (the myth was) might be reticent because their views had before not been really listened to and taken seriously by Christians from the developed countries.

The conference was divided into four sections, each of approximately a hundred people, to discuss: Economic and Social Development in World Perspective; the Nature and Function of the State in a Revolutionary Age; Structures of International Cooperation—Living Together in Peace in a Pluralistic World Society; and Man and Community in Changing Societies.

The first four meetings of these main divisions of the conference were supposed to take up the special theme assigned to each section in the light of the substance of four or five plenary addresses delivered to the conference as a whole during its first two and a half days together. These first section meetings were necessarily devoted to taking the measure of one another's thoughts, to developing *esprit,* to making no more than initial comments around the room. Consecutive discussion by which one person pushed another back upon his premises was scarcely possible in a meeting of a hundred people, at least not in these early days. Not infrequently there were a number of declarations of purity of heart on the part of the peoples among whom the Christian speaking happened to dwell on this earth, especially if their situation demands revolutionary changes in the established order.[3]

Then each section divided into three or four subsections, of eighteen to thirty-five people, each with an assigned subtopic. These subsections met six times before coming together again as a section in three final section plenaries. Each was supposed to produce approximately five pages to go into a final twenty-page section report to be proposed to the conference plenary as a "report to be received" with separate "conclusions to be adopted."

Obviously, the main work of the conference was done by these subsections. There the real debate took place, the real encounters between divergent points of view, in a setting in which there was some opportunity for our thinking to move deeper into the issues before us. Yet I must point out that the last *four* of the six times subsections met together had to be scheduled on the morning and afternoon of two days instead of on four consecutive days. By the time, therefore, subsections were less than midway into their debates and deliberations, they were seized by the necessity of drafting five pages; this had to be done in session, or sessions devoted almost exclusively to this, because there was not enough time for drafting and redrafting to be done between the last four meetings, and everything had to be agreed to and ready for translation and mimeographing to go the next day to the section for its discussion and approval. It was at this point that the Rev. George D. Younger began to say, walking to and from our subsection meetings, that our "deliberations" at Geneva should be only the beginning of a long and multifarious process of study among Christians the world over, and that the pressure should not be upon us to reach conclusions for a good many years yet on such enormous topics.

Of course, it was constantly said that we *need* not reach conclusions; if there were none, then simply none would be proposed for adoption. But that was sheer "ideology" (in the sense the conference's theological paper did not give to that much abused word), and no one who ever voiced this way of saying we were still a study conference had any reason to believe the momentum of the conference would do anything other than impel quite a number of conclusions to be reached. When we came together in section meetings,

65

it was obvious to everyone that, while a group of a hundred persons may be a deliberative body if it is a permanent body meeting together for months, it cannot engage in responsible decision making in three or four meetings. An effort was made in at least one section to preface its report by the statement that "the work of the section has been done mainly in the subsections into which we were divided, and consequently this report consists of four parts for which the members of a particular subsection are primarily responsible." If this procedure had been adopted, the unwieldly sections would simply have received and passed on the work of the smaller groups where, if anywhere, genuine debate took place for perhaps long enough time for them to take responsibility for the results. Since a number of the subsection reports had not separated out a list of "conclusions," this would have meant that the report of the sections to the conference plenary would have been without these conclusions and particular recommendations for adoption by the conference. Then the conference would have, in the main, "received" the reports of sections; and the final conference report itself would have been in a form proper only for transmission to the WCC and its member communions for their study, consideration, and action—a not inappropriate outcome, I should say, from a study conference such as was held at Geneva.

But this was not to be. The *Drang* toward agreement as to the ingredients of the problems we had faced and on particular conclusions was too strong, if for no other reason than that this was expected of the participants in their corporate capacity, no matter what reservations very many might have as individuals. So 4 x 5 pages = 20 pages of "report" the section members adopted and declared themselves responsible for recommending that the conference "receive" and make a part of its report by the same process, even though any one person had participated in the basic discussion of only one small part of it, and was even then, in the subsections, under great pressure to arrive at consensus or at an analysis of the problem too quickly.

Since it is structures and not men I am criticizing, since I affirm that more weight was put upon these procedures than they could possibly bear, since I am suggesting that from a simple inspection of what went on no one can possibly call this responsible church deliberation about a responsible society or the responsibilities of government, I can say without hesitation that the caliber of the reports is astonishingly good. The chairmen and rapporteurs of the sections deserve high praise for their accomplishment in producing, upon the basis of the work done by subsections, the final reports to be received by the conference, and in formulating, often for the first time at this late stage of the process, findings or conclusions to be recommended for adoption. In some cases this was done by lifting whole paragraphs out of the body of the shorter reports that had been written without the participants having clearly in mind (since they had only begun to debate the issues) the necessity or even the probability of drawing common conclusions. In other cases conclusions proposed to the hundred-man sections were simply formulated by the rapporteurs.

So it was that in conference plenary sessions on the last three days the 410 participants found themselves discussing thrice 118 complex, often specific judgments of fact and of value upon crucial world problems with a view to adopting, amending, or rejecting them as expressions of the thinking of the conference, statements made in its own name to the churches and to the world and transmitted to the churches for their further study and action. (At the same time the body of the reports was discussed with a view to receiving or not receiving them, together with three conference working papers, and a final "Message," the total running to a good deal more than 160 single-spaced mimeographed pages. As now printed, the text of the Official Report comes to a book in fairly fine print 210 pages in length!)

Only the most controversial recommendations or condemnations—and this means the most specific ones—were debated at any length, an individual speaker being limited to five minutes, then to three, because of the pressures of time. From time to time a speaker gained the microphone to call attention to the fact that the terms, and sometimes the spirit, in which these issues were being debated were those of a political convention and not the ones he believed appropriate to a Christian gathering. Yet on quite debatable issues from which would follow the most enormous consequences for good or ill if the leaders of state adopted the Geneva "conclusions," *never more than half* the registered participants voted in the division, usually fewer. It was clear to all that no probing debate could take place nor any substantial revision of the proposed conclusions be made in these plenary sessions. The conference was simply not a deliberative body.

Still it was possible to seize the right moment or strike the right note and prevail in voting the facts up or down or for right against the wrong and take home as a prize a phrase inserted or excised. This made it possible for the entire Indonesian delegation in the waning hours of the conference to be placed under assault, given the strong feeling on their part that they should speak responsibly *for* and *to* the entire Christian community from which they came and their feeling also that the conference should not forget to do likewise. This happened when Byron Johnson of the U.S.A. proposed an amendment to the report dealing with racial and ethnic problems which would have had the conference deplore the *"systematic persecution of the*

Chinese in Indonesia bordering on *genocide*." That, lest it be not recognized, was a reference to the recent tragic riots and senseless slaughter of communists of many races, by which a great many people in Indonesia furiously responded to the *coup* that failed. This motion was defeated only after participants from Indonesia pleaded with the conference, and among other things explained that every one of them was named in the list of vast numbers of persons to be exterminated had the *coup* succeeded, which was the sudden realization of fearful threat that prompted the slaughter.

It was possible also for a member of the British Parliament to be placed in the position of fighting for every word in a committee sent out from the final session to redraft the Rhodesian "conclusion," thus coming close to prolonging the conference beyond the time set for adjournment and the final worship service at which presumably all the work of the conference was submitted to the overruling providence of God. There is nothing wrong with "dialogue" except that this is not the way to promote it; nor responsible deliberation either, except that this was not it. Thus did the conference send out to the world a conclusion or resolution, indistinguishable from a statement proposed for further study, which pronounced that Great Britain, having failed, should turn the problem of Rhodesia over to United Nations.[4] What gives, we may ask, an assemblage of churchmen the *de jure* competence or by these procedures the *de facto* competence to decide the gritty specifics of such a problem? *The New York Times* correspondent, Anthony Lewis, could write (August 14, 1966) that the UN as it now stands can do little about Rhodesia; yet the study conference could not give calm *consideration* to such sober realities, or to the possibility that the United Nations needs no enemies so long as it has friends who wish at once and

69

without a careful review of its capabilities to load it with every otherwise insoluble or unsolved problem. There is also another sober reality which it is to be hoped Christians and others urging the UN to place Rhodesia under economic siege do not forget in taking such decision, namely, that there may be only two kinds of sanctions even under UN auspices: those that fail and those that lead to war. (Ordinarily we Christians feel free in giving particular advice so long as it is believed that there are always nonviolent solutions; and in this we do not face all the alternatives that statecraft must hold in view.) The demeaning thing for the British MP at Geneva was that he must have known that no moral authority at all could be attached by the statesmen of the world to the conclusion he was thus struggling to shape; and that whether this problem should be taken or not taken to the UN, and specifically when, had to be determined on grounds this conference was not competent *de jure* or by these procedures qualified *de facto* to assay.

It was, on the other hand, possible in the concluding plenary sessions for a statement, seriously objectionable because of what it implied, to be corrected into a meaningless one. This was the paragraph in the report on man and community which read: "There is also a feeling among the people of Asia and Africa that the U.S.A. has little hesitation to escalate the war in Vietnam because Vietnamese people are Asian." One wonders whether the United States participants were other-directed or were not effectively dialoguing, for that statement to reach the final sessions where it stood a good many procedural chances of not being excised. Did anyone propose to load the report with various statements about the feelings of people in the United States having derogatory innuendo toward the peoples of other lands and the policies of their governments?

Better still, did anyone propose that the report also state that unfortunately the *protests* in the United States against the administration's policy in Vietnam are taking on an increasing racist tone? This was, however, changed to read: "Also the escalating war in Vietnam aggravates ill feelings between races arising from the fact that Americans and others of non-Asian stock are fighting with Asians against Asians in an Asian country." [5] Only the Rev. Fred James of the U.S.A., a Negro, arose to object that in his view the statement still left standing the false assumption that United States escalation is based on racist feeling. The chairman of this section, Margaret Mead, rejected Mr. James's interpretation; she apparently preferred the by now rather senseless statement to stand. Nothing, therefore, came of this final warning, and Mr. James secured the hearing he did mainly because he declared in making that statement that he himself was opposed to our escalation. That in turn left standing—when you think about it—the assumption that had a United States participant supported the escalation, this might have been based on racist feeling. There is again nothing wrong with dialogue and responsible deliberation over issues, except that this is not the way to promote them.

Finally, it was possible for the conference to adopt as an expression of its own mind a policy decision that would be of enormous strategic and particular consequences without debate and even without notice of all that was implied. This happened when it adopted the conclusion "unanimously deploring" the fact that mainland China is "outside the United Nations," [6] taken with the paragraph in the body of the report,[7] which it is true the conference only "received," but which contained a statement about the problem of Taiwan whose legislative history was never explained to the conference. Originally this paragraph, when it came

71

from the subsection that alone could carefully consider all the issues, read: "The Churches, therefore, should endorse unequivocally the seating of the People's Republic of China in the United Nations, under the understanding that a solution be found for the *representation* of Taiwan." [8] This statement was changed by rapporteurs or by the section plenary, which could not have debated the issues adequately even if this is the correct conclusion, to read: "with the understanding that a solution be found for the *question* of Taiwan," with no mention of representation of Taiwan in the UN. This change was never explained to the conference as a whole. Thus did the conference issue in its own name recommendations about securing universal membership in the United Nations, especially on the part of China; and it accepted in ignorance as background for this a signal matter which it *might* not have wanted to receive. This surely is the way to succeed at being prophets without really trying; and because of fascination with the single-factorial issue of Red China for the church in its advice to statesmen to keep ahead of where they must be amid the gritty specifics.

I am not able to speak for the political leaders and other decision makers in society today. I can only say that a Christian theologian or ethicist would have to be out of his mind to regard the working group paper on "Theological Issues in Social Ethics" produced at the Geneva conference as *the* basis (or even *a* basis) for future discussion in any other than the trivial sense that it may on occasion be useful to start talking. It cannot be emphasized too often that the propositions affirmed by this conference, whether by receiving them or by adopting them as in either case a report of its thinking, are no more and no less than exactly that: the thinking that went on at this particular gathering, composed as it was and structured to

72

think and act as it was. Its statements have exactly the inherent meaning and importance they themselves manifest. No additional authority or persuasiveness should be attributed to them. The same statements issuing from another source would have had the same force; these same statements known to have been pondered under better deliberative conditions could be set forth in the wider human discourse of church or state with better backing; and more searching statements issuing from this or another source would have greater intrinsic force. If anyone thinks otherwise, he thinks more highly of ecumenical statements than he ought to think. If anyone persuades a church member or a civic leader otherwise, he appeals to some other authority than Scripture and right reason to bolster some partisan particularity.

The paper on "Theological Issues in Social Ethics" has to be faulted on both procedural and substantive grounds. The themes and topics on which the conference expressly set to work in sections and subsections have already been mentioned. The schedule and working time of the conference was devoted to these subjects, and to listening to plenary addresses. The Theological Working Group was, despite its title, a homeless waif. The idea was that a designated group of people already assigned to the main deliberative sections dealing with other subject matter would come together at such times as they could find for this in a tight and exhausting daily schedule, and try to bring out those theological and ethical perspectives found to be quite indispensable in the discussion of those other topics. This would be the way to lift up to view the theology and social ethics of the conference, i.e., the foundations of Christian social ethics today, if the conference succeeded in stating such an ethics.

I should say that the idea was to do Christian theology and ethics by induction and infiltration. Again, with all respect for the individuals involved in this, and for their capabilities, this is simply not the way to advance the cause or deepen and broaden the base of ecumenical theology and ethics. Since the method of doing ethics was set up to be contextual, it is not at all surprising that the theology and ethics resulting from this were contextual in the extreme. No stream rises higher than its source.

This also says something about the mini-Christian analysis of those urgent problems of politics and economics to which the attention of the conference was exclusively directed. It is not surprising that a narrowly contextual ethic can be the only insight to come from (by methodical pre-arrangement) doing Christian ethics contextually and by induction from perspectives needed in the solution of problems. So also if the Christian analysis of world political and economic problems is set up to be without primary attention to Christian theology and ethics, then it is not at all surprising that the resulting reports and conclusions on these questions read for so much of the way as if they could have issued from many another world gathering of concerned liberals. It was advertently or inadvertently designed to be that way: in other than Christian *terms*.

One evening plenary session at Geneva was set aside for addresses on the topic "The Relevance of Theology to the Social Revolutions of Our Time." These addresses were supposed to inform and fructify the discussion and debates at Geneva. They helped in theologically informing the conference in only a meager degree (even as the evening of plenary addresses on the nuclear problem constituted no substantial input for the mind of the conference on the latter question). The theologians spoke instead on a topic not assigned them, which may be formulated to read: "The

74

Relevance of Revolution to the Theology of Our Time." As Professor Franklin Sherman of the Chicago Lutheran Seminary has written, each of the three speakers (H. D. Wendland of Münster, Richard Shaull of Princeton Theological Seminary, and Archpriest Vitaly Borovoy of Leningrad and Geneva) appeared to have "interpreted his task as that of emphasizing *relevance* and interpreting the *revolutions* more than expositing the *theology* that was supposed to be relevant to the said revolutions. They had gotten the underlining in their titles in the wrong place. The result was that the conference suffered from a serious theological vitamin deficiency." [9] I shall argue in a moment that the "theology" of the conference was a truncated Barthianism. A reason for the truncation was that the conference began with "man's disorder" (or man's revolutionary prospects) rather than with "God's design" (as Barth said of Amsterdam) ; and of necessity one cannot go very far in "prolonging" *that* into theological ethics even if he is accustomed to disciplined reflection.

It has to be reported that when the paper on "Theological Issues in Social Ethics" came before the conference there were the strongest calls for us to "have the courage to do what we do too little at ecumenical conferences, namely, say nothing at all when we cannot say something adequately." There was a motion to refer back especially the first part with its astonishing interpretation of Genesis and its identification of the "creation" with empirically observable "nature," as not a suitable starting point for ecumenical discussion. But then it was pointed out that if we began doing this the conference would have to apologize for much else besides. One of the Russians declared that since this was not dogma and all else is free, the conference could receive anything and resolute as it pleased. Even a move to insert the words "conscious of the fact that the working group was under great difficulty in the performance of its task" was defeated.

I would say the paper might not have been received into the report of the conference if it had not been for the feeling that this would be (a) unfair, since this had not been the action in the case of other reports or parts of reports; and if it had not been for the feeling that referral back would have been (b) useless, since there was not time for another paper to be prepared and submitted, and obviously something *had* to be said about Theology and Ethics by the 1966 Geneva Conference on Church and Society. Therefore, we pushed principles aside and did the right thing contextually. The conference refused to say nothing at all, knowing this had not been said at all adequately. For such procedural reasons I affirm that no Christian theologian or ethicist can henceforth say, except in the most trivial sense, that the theological paper provides a basis for discussion or a proper or helpful beginning for discussion. And I suggest that the churches and churchmen and the leaders of institutions and of men in society generally who were addressed by Geneva 1966 on any number of subjects have abundant procedural grounds for saying the same thing about what was said to them on other subjects as well.

I must be brief in stating the chief substantive issue raised by acceptance of the theological paper. The "theology" of the conference was a christological-eschatologial dynamic monism. The elevation of this began when John Bennett made the decision to place Richard Shaull's chapter first and most prominent among the essays in the preparatory volume *Christian Social Ethics in a Changing World*.[10] Rather, the deliberate narrowing of ecumenical theology and ethics began when Professor Shaull, who teaches ecumenics at Princeton Theological Seminary, adopted as a theological method or criterion to test the truth of orthodoxy, neo-orthodoxy, and ecumenical theology the question whether this any longer has appeal to some young revolutionaries he has known and admires.

The revolutionary theology pervasive at the conference was, of course, a truncated Barthianism,[11] stressing Christ and the revolutionary situation, lopping off Barth's own "prolongation" of his Christocentric ethics into a doctrine of man and of creation and many a principle and structure in his "special ethics." Expansive as the feelings may be of those who possess this theology in one or another of its generational versions, the fact is that such an organization of the Christian understanding of life and of politics under the second article of the Creed only (reducing the first, "creation," to the processes of historicized "nature" and the third to Christ's ever coming present triumph over the powers) manifests a quite definite narrowing of the bases of ecumenical theology. Those churches that believe there is some logic to the order and sequence among the heads of the Creed (that there is Creation, Law and Ordinances, then Gospel, and that only with the end of time will Christ triumph over all the powers) could no longer find a place in the ecumenical movement they have known or in the discussions of the meaning of "a responsible society" by this or any other name. So the lines are drawn: between assertedly contextual revolutionary-Christocentric eschatologism and ecumenical theology to date. The future of the WCC depends on the moderation or the meeting of this challenge.

The same substantial narrowness that threatens the existing ecumenical theology and ethics (if theologians of the church had any reason to regard the theology of Geneva 1966 as the basis for future discussion) would also make quite impossible the development of a broader and deeper ecumenical theology in dialogue with the Roman Catholic Church post–Vatican II.

This was made clear to us at Geneva by one of the Roman Catholic observers in the section on the role of the state. The issue he broached was settled in open disregard for ecumenical ethics and the future of Christ's whole church which, one would have supposed, should claim attention at a conference on Church and Society at least equal to the claims of the immediate need (as some suppose), for reconstructing all Christian categories in view of the revolutionary needs of the hour. Instead of asking for help in formulating our documents so that they might open windows in the direction of a still wider ecumenical ethics (which was the treatment accorded Protestant observers at the Vatican Council), in this instance at Geneva there seemed to be a relentless determination to replace a term that allowed for the narrow as well as for a broader meaning by one that was *believed* to exclude the broader meaning. This was done by "legal" parliamentary means; yet, I think, this showed the procedural dubiety of those means and the unlikelihood they could result in sound common thinking.

Subsection 3 of Section II on the role of the state was charged with saying something about law and lawmaking. This group was composed of a number of theologians, philosophers of law, and lawyers from a wide variety of countries. Its discussion centered upon the relation between law and morality; and I venture to say that there took place in this group more sustained debate about theological foundations than anywhere else in the conference. The results were two connected paragraphs on "The Theological Basis of Law" that went into the larger section report.[12] The second paragraph opened with a bridge sentence, "Christians find in the idea of the person the integral focus of all questions of freedom, justice, peace and equality."

When this was brought before the hundred-man section to be adopted as its report, an attack was mounted against the word "person," and this was changed to "person-in-community," in a hurried meeting and necessarily without adequate thought.

It is to be noted that the next sentence went on to say, "Persons-in-community under God are never in a static situation"; and that the word "person" in the first sentence *permitted* anyone who believes that persons are only persons-in-community, or are this to the whole extent of their beings, to place that construction upon it. But since the word "person" permitted other and broader meanings to be assigned to what the sentence affirmed to be the integral focus of freedom, justice, etc., this was felt to be incompatible with the outlook of revolutionary monism. It was at this point that Professor Michael Fogarthy of the University College of South Wales called the section's attention to the fact that the person transcends his communities and that ecumenical Christian thought would be beating retreat if we did not say so. He even gave a revolutionary twist to this classic assertion, saying that if this were not so, men could not have the leverage radically to transform and revolutionize their communities. To no avail. The person must be regarded as *in situ* in order to be dynamically and unavoidably in a revolutionary situation; this is the way today to speak for man. Even to *allow* another conception of man would be too great a concession to the "ideology" of the constitutionalism of the developed countries of the Northern Hemisphere.

Thus was a door closed instead of windows opened in the direction of a further development of ecumenical ethics in cooperation with Roman Catholicism.[13] At the same time, a limited meaning was given to the theological terms used in the preceding paragraph, since these come to focus, it was said, in an understanding of the person and his justice and freedom. That paragraph speaks of "Christian anthropology, our faith in God as creator, in Christ as redeemer, and in the Holy Spirit," man in the image of God, etc., in such a way as to include those churches that believe there is a logic in the order of the heads of the Creed, but without excluding a church theologian who may want to make one or another concentration in a single head but who yet wants seriously to talk about man, creation, and justice. Thus the same stroke that closed windows to the Roman Catholic personalism that has been so vital in and after the Vatican Council also narrowed the bases of our existing ecumenical theology and social ethics.

All this on the assumption that anyone has any grounds for believing what was said in the final report. To the contrary, there is every reason to fault the wisdom of formulations adopted by such procedures. In this case the movement to effect this change came, of course, from participants who had not done the real work of discussing the theological issues. It came, in fact, largely from participants in another subsection who had been charged with discussing the task of the state in developing nations in their search for viable political structures, with the encouragement of some members of the "American curia" who want to effect this slanting of ecumenical social ethics just as passionately as anyone from the "South." Ironically, the same block of participants who in section plenary succeeded in introducing this fundamental change into the report of another subsection was the same block that threw the conference plenary into something of an uproar and held up acceptance of its own section's report because they believed that in the final drafting of it too many changes had been made in that part which they as a subsection had been mainly responsible for debating and formulating. (This too

80

brief debate was over the relation of the Army to "nation building"—which I thought to be a great idea to bring home to western constitutionalists and against ritualistic liberal opponents of United States support of any and all military regimes.)

None of the foregoing is intended to say who was right on this or that point, as too quickly the deliberations of smaller groups became section reports and finally the report of the conference itself. The conclusion to be drawn is rather that there was some measure of deliberation in the eighteen to thirty-five man subsections; the participants in these groups did the real work and made themselves in a degree responsible for what they said. If this had been the design of the conference, the subgroups could have met together more often and could have said what was said far better on the several important themes assigned them. This would have been worth sending forward for continuing study, and worth transmitting to subsequent "policy" meetings of the WCC and of its member denominations. There would have been better statements to cite. But then it would have been altogether too clear that the group being cited was only the eighteen to thirty-five persons who happened to comprise these groups, and no one would think of adding *that* authority to the wisdom or lack of wisdom inherent in their words. That the section plenaries or the conference plenaries *said anything after deliberation* is a chimera and a procedural hoax. The intent of the foregoing is therefore to say that no one *should* ever cite the authority of Geneva 1966, or add anything to the wisdom or lack of wisdom in the words of its report. The conclusions of the conference are for discussion and properly should be discussed; but as such they do not constitute, except in a trivial sense, *the* basis or *a* basis for future discussion or for the formation of ecumenical ethics or public policy.

2. The most "newsworthy" conclusion of the conference was its statement that recent United States actions in Vietnam "cannot be justified." We need now to examine these paragraphs[14] and their legislative history. The religion reporter of *The New York Times*,[15] Edward B. Fiske, interpreted the criticism of American policies in Vietnam as reflecting "not only a concern for peace but also a fundamental shift of the balance of power within the World Council of Churches" by the influx of "former mission churches" and the presence at the conference of so many churchmen from the developing or undeveloped countries, and particularly from the Southern Hemisphere. The confrontation between East and West has now been replaced by the confrontation between North and South, and this is what asserted itself at Geneva.

So far as the statement on Vietnam is concerned, nothing could be farther from the truth. That conclusion was "made in America," or at least in the North.

The initial committee appointed to draft a first formulation of a statement on Vietnam consisted of an *observer* at the conference, Dr. Homer Jack, U.S.A., who has been notably identified with the activities of SANE, and Bishop Tibor Bartha of the Reformed Church of Hungary. One may pause here to reflect upon the influence on the possible outcome accorded to an observer at the conference when it was a question of dealing in specifics of political and military policy. This was surely far greater than that granted to observers by their right to speak and greater than that denied them by having no right to vote and no practical possibility of speaking in the final conference plenary sessions. The reason for pausing to reflect on this is not to say there was anything wrong in Homer Jack's possible influence upon the statement on Vietnam. The present writer, who also was not a "participant," was extended the possibility of an equal influence upon the subsection report on law and lawmaking. I mention this detail for two reasons only: (1) to point to the irony in the fact that it was possible for the influence of a nonparticipant to be exerted upon a particular political pronouncement (even though the first draft was rejected) while a Roman Catholic observer, as I have indicated, failed to be able to prevent a narrowing of the theological and ethical bases of another section report. And (2) this is simply my first proof of the fact that the statement on Vietnam was an East-West product; whether it was a compromise depends on how much the westerners dialogued or on whether they went to Geneva to obtain the conclusion that was adopted. There was nothing wrong in the way statements were evolved if one accepts the premise that the thinking of this conference has only internal accreditation within the limits of the structures and procedures that were used.

The second informal committee that actually drafted the three crucial paragraphs, and defended them against all revision or amendment until they finally became the conclusion of the conference, consisted of four persons: Professor John Bennett, President of Union Theological Seminary in New York; Metropolitan Nicodim of the Russian Orthodox Church; Albert Laham, a lawyer from Lebanon; and an observer from India, A. K. Thampy, businessman. The statement read:

105. In the light of the above considerations, we have repeatedly emphasized the tragic situation in Vietnam. We would suggest that the churches have a special obligation to question continually the wisdom and rightness of the present Vietnam policies of the belligerents. We welcome the action of the World Council of Churches and its Commission of the Churches

83

on International Affairs aimed at restoring peace in Vietnam and at stopping the bombing of the North by the United States and South Vietnam, and the military infiltration of the South by North Vietnam.

106. However, the massive and growing American military presence in Vietnam and the long-continued bombing of villages in the South and of targets a few miles from cities in the North cannot be justified. They involve the danger of escalation of the war into a world conflict and do not bring South Vietnam closer to political stability or solve the problems which have produced a revolutionary situation in that country.

107. In view of the dangers created by this situation, we urge that all hostilities and military activity be stopped and that the conditions be created for the peaceful settlement of the Vietnam problem through the United Nations, or the participants in the Geneva Conference, or other international agencies.

Whether these paragraphs were only made in the North or also in America depends on whether the participant from the United States wanted any other result. Whether it was a compromise depends on whether he wanted the statement to say something it did not, or objected to something it said. This may have been the case; John Bennett's well-honed ecumenical spirit may have prevented a far more extreme statement on Vietnam from being proposed to the conference. The discussion that went on in the two or three hours this committee had to prepare its draft was, of course, not common knowledge at the conference, nor a part of its legislative history. But would it not be a fair conclusion from John Bennett's recent writings on United States policy in Vietnam to say, at least, that he likely did not do battle for a statement that would speak for the entire church in America as passionately as Mr. Laham later pleaded with the conference not to say what it wanted to say about antisemitism in a way that, he believed, did not take account of the special position and responsibilities of Christians in an Arab land like Lebanon? Indeed one can discern, I judge, the fine hand of John Bennett in these paragraphs taken as a whole.

The first paragraph was a balanced package of particular political condemnations addressed to both sides. "The churches," it affirmed, "have a special obligation to question continually the wisdom and rightness of the present Vietnam policies of the belligerents." Then followed a reference to the action of the Central Committee of the WCC and its CCIA on February 16, 1966, calling for "stopping the bombing of the North by the United States and South Vietnam, and of the military infiltration of the South by North Vietnam."

It was explained during the brief conference debate over the next controversial paragraph that it was meant to build upon what was said in the first paragraph, that what had been said in disapproval of the infiltration of the South was *presupposed,* and that the second paragraph was meant only to take into account events since the WCC statement on February 16, 1966. Yet there can be no doubt that in paragraph 106 a judicious balancing of specific recommendations and censures became unstuck. We have noted that the telegram sent to Visser 't Hooft and O. Frederick Nolde on July 1, 1966, also made reference to the February statement, and went on to address itself to subsequent events. It also voiced demands upon United States policy that assume that the Administration could still make peace even though Hanoi had not responded favorably to the February call by stopping the infiltration. Yet, in doing this, there can be no doubt that the telegram took more fully and fairly into account what had happened since February 16, and the political and military realities it nevertheless bypassed, than the Geneva Conference did. Before making additional pleas or censures, the telegram said: "We appreciate that the United States has offered to stop bombing North Vietnam on condition that North Vietnam cease infiltration of the South and deeply regret that no affirmative response has been forthcoming." During the summer, 1966, the realities were that Hanoi precisely was not going to agree to mutual de-escalation of the war, of both the bombing and the infiltration.[16] Both the telegram and the Geneva Conference statement, and the latter with less realism and accuracy, are examples of how to succeed at particular political prophecy without really trying: when one set of recommendations fails, one has only to up the ante on one side only, and one will still be prophesying peace where there is no peace. Thus did the statement in Geneva go on to affirm that "the massive and growing American military presence in Vietnam and the long continued bombing of villages in the South and of targets a few miles from cities in the North cannot be justified."

There was a brief, spirited debate in the conference plenary over whether the words "cannot be justified" should be changed to "are to be condemned." This was proposed as a strengthening of the paragraph. It was defeated, among other things, by the assertion by one of the leaders of the section, Archpriest Borovoy of Leningrad and Geneva, that "cannot be justified" is, in fact, stronger language, since it means "cannot under any circumstances or by any argument be justified." There was no argument made for this proposition, or for how this particular group of churchmen could know this, or knew there were no justifying reasons. It is reported that John Bennett thought that the phrase "cannot be justified" was more reasoned and thoughtful and hence had greater impact than the more hotheaded "condemned." True, this phrase *suggests* a more reasoned position. But in the logic of the matter it would have required an extraordinary effort to demonstrate that *universal negative* proposition, and this was scarcely undertaken. The successful defense of it, however, made it possible for some news reports to say that the conference beat back an attempt to "condemn" United States actions in Vietnam, and only decreed that they could not be justified. Headlines the next day in *The New York Times,* however, announced to all the world that the WCC Conference had "condemned" all these things the United States is doing, no doubt about it—and with no corrective recognition of the military initiatives the United States is (rightly or wrongly) continuing to face.

The final of the three paragraphs redresses the balance by urging "that all hostilities and military activity be stopped and that the conditions be created for the peaceful settlement of the Vietnam problem through the United Nations, or the participants in the Geneva Conference, or other international agencies." Insofar as that is a particular recommendation, it is an appeal to sources of action that the United States would clearly be willing to try to bring about conditions in which the United States can responsibly stop the bombing and all the other things it is doing that are condemned unilaterally in paragraph 106. Insofar as the final paragraph is a return to a balanced set of appeals to the belligerents to stop all hostilities, it is tantamount to a generality like "Let there be peace," since this is still a world (the nation-state system) and Vietnam is a place where it takes two to make peace.

The successful defense of these paragraphs from all amendment through all the stages of deliberation prior to the conference plenary which adopted them as its "conclusions" went something like this. Max Kohnstamm, from Holland, who delivered the most politically informed address and at the same time the most thoroughly Christian

87

address to the problems of international politics that was given at the conference, proposed that the two sentences comprising paragraph 106 be conflated to read: "The massive and growing American military presence in Vietnam and the long-continued bombing of villages in the South and of targets a few miles from cities in the North involve the danger of escalation of the war into a world conflict and do not bring South Vietnam closer to political stability or solve the problems which have produced a revolutionary situation in that country." That would have turned the unilateral condemnation of recent United States actions into a warning or a mere statement of fact. Whenever this was proposed, or anyone else moved to amend the committee's original draft so as to moderate it in any way, Metropolitan Nicodim of Russia (one of the drafters) would say that he disagreed substantially with the proposed statement anyway and if it was changed in any respect that did not "strengthen" it there would be no report, or *two* reports. On the other hand, whenever anyone proposed to make the statement more extreme, Kohnstamm would say that if this were done there would have to be no report, or two. Thus Nicodim found himself in the ironic position of defending a "milder" draft against the desire of a number of more radical Americans that the statement "condemn" the United States government; and in this he was joined by John Bennett. In the midst of this standoff and these altercations, Bishop Sarkissian of Lebanon, one of the conference presidents, would draw attention to one way of avoiding them: namely, by remembering that the WCC and the conference are not obliged to get so specific. These were words sent out over the waters to return to him void.

Perhaps there was value in thus protecting these paragraphs from all attacks. Despite the imbalance in the statement on this conflict that was introduced by paragraph 106, perhaps the conference said what it had to say. But this judgment depends altogether on the value one places on erecting a consensus and on the estimate one has of the Church and Society Syndrome that allows councils of churchmen, meeting as such, to indulge in particular pronouncements, resolutions, or conclusions on complex political questions, ultimate responsibility for which belongs to citizens and the magisterial office. Not even the "magisterium" of the Roman Catholic Church has in recent centuries, if ever, gone so far in telling statesmen what is required of them. The shock of producing no report on the Vietnam question, or two contradictory specific reports, might have been salutory. This might have driven home the truth that amid the gritty specifics, the crunch of political forces, and clashes among the justices of men there are two sides to this and to most world political and economic questions to which Christians can with equal sincerity adhere, and whose consciences ought not to be faulted—or even *seem* to be faulted if they disagree—by the use of such strong words for any of these particulars as "cannot be justified" by a gathering, sponsored by the churches, of Christians who can only speak for themselves. Then, instead of the balanced set of specific condemnations becoming unstuck, it would have been this fascination with decision-making exercises that would have been proved void.

We need, finally, to examine more closely that most controversial paragraph 106. It may be that the argument for saying that the bombing of targets a few miles from cities in the North cannot be justified was contained in the next sentence: *because* of the danger of escalation of the war into a world conflict. It may be that the argument for saying that the long-continued bombing of villages in the South cannot be justified was likewise contained in this same sentence: *because* this does not bring South Vietnam closer to political stability or solve the problems that have produced a revolutionary situation in that country. There was, indeed, considerable virtue in Kohnstamm's proposal that these two sentences be put together and welded into a judgment of fact, with only the implication that if the facts be so, then such actions cannot be justified. But what, we may ask, gave the Geneva Conference *de jure* or *de facto* competence to render any such judgments of fact? On the first, the real determiners of United States policy have to estimate the *degree* of danger of escalation into world conflict; and, having done so, they have to compare this with the danger of world conflict if some other course of action is taken or if there is no military action at all in South Vietnam or in the rest of Southeast Asia. Doubtless this depends on the political picture one has of the world, but what accredits the churchmen's picture against that of the government's as a justifying reason?

On the second, no one ever said that the military destruction taking place in the South is contributing anything positive to political stability or to solving the problems which have produced a revolutionary situation in that country, but only that this may stop the destruction of the fragile village and central governmental structures by Viet Cong military action, and may bring to an end the "contribution" they are making to the solving of South Vietnam's social problems by killing village officials, school teachers, food distributors, doctors, and others. This much, and this much only, can be granted: Geneva 1966 might well have made the statements of fact Kohnstamm wanted it to make, if these had been prefaced by words like "We warn that." This would have called attention to the specific danger, and to the specific need for positive social reconstruction. This would have been far short of an assertion of certainty concerning a specific reading of the facts, and even more remote from the claim to certain moral knowledge, indeed the self-righteousness, in the statement that recent United States actions cannot by any argument be justified to the consciences of reasonable men.

In a sense there is not much point in making the foregoing argument. As debated at Geneva the two sentences of paragraph 106 were two separately numbered paragraphs (subsequently made into a single paragraph by the final drafting committee). The injustice or the condemnation of recent United States actions in Vietnam was debated at Geneva as formulated in that single naked assertion. To some the statement as formulated seemed reasonable and thoughtful; to others it seemed weak for this reason, or because expressed in the negative. In either case, it was largely unsupported by rational moral argument. Still, there may have been many who thought the grounds for the condemnation were supplied by the next sentence (then, the following paragraph); and we have now seen the answer that could be made to this viewpoint. In the danger of escalation and in the fact that the military action taking place in the South is no substitute for the economic action and political solutions that are also needed, there was set forth some ground— let us say, even, a good deal of support—for the controversial unilateral condemnation. The question remains whether these considerations are *sufficient* reason for compelling the conclusion that recent United States actions in Vietnam "cannot be justified" by any line of conscientious political reasoning. In the nature of the case there could be no conclusive proof of such an exclusive proposition. Here can simply be seen the wisdom of the proverb: One man's relevance may be another man's betrayal.

Moreover, as written, paragraph 106 does not remove, indeed it comes close to suggesting, an interpretation of its meaning that would be quite, quite in error. Does it or does it not imply that "the long-continued bombing of villages" is the *design* of the war against the insurgents, that villages are deliberately bombed as a matter of policy and not because they are Viet Cong strongholds; and that *for this reason* recent United States actions cannot be justified? Does the statement, or does it not, imply that only interdiction targets like bridges on the road to the South and not oil storage tanks near cities are legitimate military targets; and that *for this reason* recent United States actions cannot be justified? What "Hanoi" or a "village" means may be very clear; but it seems difficult for a great many people in the semantically confused Western world to get to know the meaning of *"bombing* Hanoi" or *"bombing* villages." Did Geneva add to this confusion? This is not clear. On the other hand, if this was not the meaning or a meaning permitted by the wording, then the conference had finally only a *quantitative* judgment to make about this war and has only quantitative judgments to make about justice in the conduct of any war. It said only that more destruction is always worse, de-escalation always better. Even if a political leader listens to such a word from churchmen in a particular instance, he is bound to reply, "That depends—on the destructiveness of a longer war or of the other real options in the long run." Much better was the politically and militarily *relevant* statement of the Vatican Council, "Any act of war aimed indiscriminately at the destruction of entire cities or of extensive areas along with their population is crime against God and man himself. It merits unequivocal and unhesitating condemnation." [17] This did not presume to supplant the responsibility of political office in saying what this means in specific practice or in the way nations are presently organized for war or in riposte to the way insurgents choose to fight in their resorts to arms.

3. Here may be inserted an account of "some activities of U.S. citizens acting as individuals during the conference on the matter of Vietnam." [18] These were discussed in several meetings of United States participants, and others present at Geneva in any capacity, called to discuss "follow up." I attended two of these meetings at which, in addition to the plans of the NCC and of the various member denominations, the chief action discussed was a telegram to President Johnson occasioned especially by the news of Hanoi's threat to try captured American flyers and execute them for "war crimes." There were indications in the press that some of our political leaders wanted United States response in that event to be grim indeed, or feared that it would be. So did we. Many wanted a telegram protesting American involvement and escalation in Vietnam, as well as warning against reprisals in excess or in kind if the prisoners were executed. After considerable discussion it was generally agreed that the telegram be directed to the more limited and immediate issue. Such a telegram was sent, signed by seventy-five United States citizens present at the conference.

The interesting thing was how difficult it was for this group of American Christians to come to terms with the meaning of "reprisals," and to decide what alone should be said if we wanted to say something that by a long shot might be politically relevant. I argued that the wording could only condemn any act of reprisal upon populations or upon prisoners held by the United States or South Vietnam, since in this world of nation-states the enforcement of international conventions and especially any limits upon the conduct of war or upon the treatment of prisoners depends on the threat of reprisals of some sort. This was to say that we should warn against reprisals of a certain kind, of an inherently unjustifiable kind, deliberately upon populations or upon prisoners of war in our own power. Roger Shinn argued that if the event we feared occurred we should, in our telegram, leave the President something to do, because he was bound to have to do something. Even if military actions the next day had been planned long before, they would be signaled as reprisals.

This bit of "legalism" from Ramsey and this political "realism" from Shinn had only some effect on the wording of the telegram; but, I judged, sufficient effect. In addition to a sentence reading, "The current episode involving American prisoners should not be made the occasion for any acts of reprisal," a sentence was inserted after that which read, "We deplore any suggestion that we lay waste the cities of North Vietnam." And instead of saying in the concluding sentence that "acts of vengeance *and reprisals* . . ." it was said that "acts of vengeance are abhorrent to Christian conscience and inimical to national and world interest." This permitted some of the seventy-five persons who signed the telegram, and paid one Swiss franc to send it, to construe that the words "lay waste their cities" controlled the meaning of "acts of reprisal." Doubtless many signed it because they wanted to censure reprisals as such, of any kind. Such ambiguity is the price of togetherness.

There was not, however, the same breadth of meaning in the opening sentence, which simply said that "we the undersigned Americans are more keenly aware than ever before of church and world criticism and anguish over United States involvement and escalation of conflict in Vietnam." One American did say that this sentence alone would have prevented his signing, on the ground that, if we wanted to do something politically effective, we should not begin with a sentence that, in the unlikely event that it reached to the President and he began reading it, would cause him to stop at that point because of a *possible* implication that there was not concern and anguish over this involvement on his and every American's part, and because of the *actual* implication that the conflict has been escalated by the United States alone, internal to a statement of fact about the American delegation's awareness. That man is quite knowledgeable in foreign affairs, and the formation of public policy. He apparently follows the old school maxim attributed to J. H. Oldham, "Find out where the power is, and lunch with it," and not the current maxim of Christian social action, "Find out where the power is, and confront it—even ritualistically." But that first sentence was only a statement of the American delegation's awareness, and I thought it a true statement, however surprising that anyone would have to go to Geneva thus to be made aware. If there were any who signed the telegram because they wanted to *protest* American involvement and escalation of conflict in Vietnam, that was their opinion. The telegram was narrowly addressed to the danger of reprisals; and only here was there a degree of ambiguity—concerning whether we meant to say that no act or only some acts of reprisal could not be justified.

Then what happened? In the first place, the document announcing these several activities on the part of United States citizens at the conference, made available to all the other persons in attendance, placed in its first paragraph to sum up the sense of the telegram only the sentence that said "the current episode involving prisoners should not be made the occasion for any act of reprisal." This was not quite up to the best journalistic standards for writing a first paragraph. It was, however, a minor point; and the wording of the entire telegram was at the bottom of the page.

Far more serious was the telegram sent at the same time

95

to the Foreign Minister of North Vietnam over the signature of Jon L. Regier, associate general secretary for Christian Life and Mission for the NCC (under whose supervision now falls the International Affairs Commission and the churches' special action for peace headed by Robert Bilheimer). This telegram began by saying that "at the WCC Conference on Church and Society seventy-five Americans present had cabled President Johnson *protesting* United States involvement in and any escalation of the conflict in Vietnam." It went on, of course, to urge Hanoi "to initiate or respond to opportunities for negotiation" of a settlement to the conflict, and to urge that "captured personnel held by any country be treated according to standards set by the International Red Cross," and specifically the captured American flyers. But I believe the damage had been committed by that first sentence. If there is any government in the world today that is likely to listen to seventy-five churchmen from the United States, stating that they have protested from a world podium against American involvement in and escalation of the conflict in Vietnam, it is the regime in Hanoi! If this telegram to the Foreign Minister of North Vietnam had any effect upon that government, it was not likely on the matter of the treatment of captured personnel, but in the direction of steeling Hanoi against negotiations now and the prolongation of the present, tragic arbitrament of arms in South Vietnam. If I thought telegrams from churchmen and academics have much effect upon governments, I could not now avoid protesting against having been made to have a small degree of complicity in an action at Geneva that may have been war-prolonging and death-dealing.[19] My purpose is, instead, to show the complexion and tenor of the American participants at the conference; and let no one say that this was derived from dialogue or from entirely novel experiences with which we were confronted there.

I have a brief comment on the letter addressed to Bishop Reuben Mueller, President of the NCC, signed by eight individual United States churchmen.[20] While this was an action of a group of individuals, the letter began by saying, quite correctly, that "many of our fellow churchmen of the U. S. present at the Conference on Church and Society . . . have asked us to convey to you their anguish over the U. S. Government's position in Vietnam." The idea that there should be such a letter was, in fact, on the agenda when the Americans present at the conference were first convened by Dr. Jon L. Regier; a draft of the letter was distributed to us when we first met; and in any case it was impossible to discuss all the ramifications of doing this even if there had been inclination to do so. For a certainty, the movement to send this letter did not arise from dialogue with our fellow Christians from around the world. It was the other way around. It was conjoined with what was called dialogue with them. Geneva was used as a site from which to secure leverage upon the NCC that was already felt to be needed. This letter, then, addressed to the topmost voices and "power structure" of the NCC, may be compared with the *Christian Century–Christianity and Crisis* editorial "A Joint Appeal to the National Council of Churches" [21] pinpointed at a lower echelon, namely, "the NCC—represented by its Commission on International Affairs," whose leadership was praised in the area of "generalized issues" but found wanting "regarding the difficult concrete questions." It can scarcely be doubted that, whatever may be wrong or lethargic about the NCC and its member denominations, the writers of that editorial and one year later the letter to Bishop Mueller already had in mind the specific conclusion or conclusions they believed should be reached.

97

This in any case is clear from the letter. "It is our conviction," the signers said, "that the NCC should take immediate and decisive steps to mobilize the resources of the Council and its constituent denominations to bring the necessity for reassessment [of our Government's involvement in Vietnam] before the President of the United States, the Secretaries of State and Defense, the appropriate congressional committees, and the American public." [22] Here the call is not for the churches in America, the entire church, to go through any reassessment, through a dialogue that has amplitude, of what we should be saying to the world or to churchmen. The call is not for the social action curial structure of the NCC and its member denominations to make an agonizing reappraisal of whether in always speaking to the church it is rightly speaking *for* the church. Instead, the call is "to mobilize the resources" as they exist and are in the habit of working, but doubtless to search also for new methods, to bring the necessity for reassessment of the government's involvement in Vietnam before everybody who has responsibility for making these decisions and before every citizen. This includes many a Christian who ought not to have his conscience faulted because he believes otherwise. Yet the letter spoke only of the *necessity* for radically reappraising United States involvement in Vietnam, and swaying the government thereto, premising that there can be no question but that this policy is *wrong;* the letter said exactly what the Geneva Conference said: This "cannot be justified." Who can doubt that this will in the follow up be cited as authority for swaying the American public, even though the conference spoke only for itself through deliberative processes that were not very apt? All this is to try to make government responsible on a predetermined definition of the meaning of this drawn from procedures that can hardly be described as a responsible church speaking. This comes from driving too deeply into one's soul the role of always speaking to the church, and the idea that specific policy-making exercises are events in salvation history when these are done by churchmen.

Finally, there was a response made by the American participants to the address to the conference by Professor Yoshiaki Iisaka of Japan. His address on "Peace in a Nuclear Age" ended with an account of the delegation of Japanese who, on the initiative of the church in Japan, came to the United States to engage in discussion with Christians in America on the issue of Vietnam. It was believed that there should be a "conclusion" of the conference calling for the inauguration of many such delegations, running in both or all directions, "for the purpose of conversation and dialogue on matters of war and peace as an expression of love and our interdependent relationships," in order for the world Christian community to broaden and deepen its witness to one another and in order that the church come into being in its ecumenical reality with some transcendence over the partial points of view of the peoples of earth among whom we dwell. It was further thought that it would be an excellent gesture and more than a gesture of our adherence to true dialogue if a participant from the United States proposed this as an amendment at an appropriate point in the plenary discussion of the reports. Professor Charles V. Willie of Syracuse University was asked to do this for us.

The motion was made and carried. The shocking thing was, however, for anyone who came to Geneva wanting and ready for dialogue, what Professor Willie said in speaking to this motion. "It is not midnight yet in the Vietnam war," he began. "But the hour is late. . . . And so, Mr. Chairman, we are knocking on the door of the nations of the world, and asking them to help us before it is too

late." Then came an attribution that "my fellow countrymen
. . . shared my sentiments" last night (which may have been
true enough), and that this was what we had asked him
to say (which was not). "We want our people to hear
what we have heard. . . . We want you to tell us about
the ravages of war and the way to world peace and brother-
hood."

That is the way to achieve the transcendence of the church
by other-directedness and one-way dialogue even if delegations move in all directions. If this is any indication of what
went on at Geneva—and I believe it is—then there was
nothing very dialogic about it. By and large, the American
participants, composed too largely of the social action curias,
clergymen and academics, brilliant youth one rarely met at
the Methodist Youth Fellowship, and with no Christian
laymen whose vocation it is actually to share in policy-
making executive leadership in the aspired responsible society, did not come to startling new awareness. By and
large, they saw or thought they saw their own reflections
in the mirror. Can anyone doubt that if delegations are
actually sent back and forth across national boundaries this
will not be to exchange perspectives or even to broaden
and deepen our understanding with a view to determining
a whole range of too specific proposals to make to the
world; but rather (as both the letter to Bishop Mueller and
Professor Willie said) to "mobilize resources" for enforc-
ing a predetermined specific policy upon fellow Christians
and fellow citizens whose consciences may be otherwise,
and upon decision makers who alone *can* in their deliberations count all the cost/benefits[23] and who alone must bear
the responsibility if this should prove disastrous? Professor
Kenneth Boulding, economist at the University of Michi-
gan, was of the opinion that advertently or inadvertently
the conference was rigged not to be able to hear fully and

100

favorably the case that can be made for the values of some version of classical liberal economics in nation building and in world economic development.[24] Something like that is my opinion concerning the position the conference came to on Vietnam. Kenneth Boulding would disagree with me on this; he was one of the signers of the letter to Bishop Mueller.

His name there leads me to say, finally, that there was a point worth contemplating in a proposal he made to the conference. Noting the remarkable and fruitful dialogue between Christians and Marxists in Europe, and not only in communist lands, Boulding pointed out that nothing like this would be possible in the United States, or at least nothing as significant, because there are so few Marxists. The parallel to this for us, he said, would be if steps were taken to open dialogue between the liberal church opinion represented in the NCC and the conservative evangelicals—the right wing.

The concluding point to be made here is that this suggestion is startling because it is. And it is startling because in the United States conservative and liberal *religious* opinion is the same thing as conservative and liberal *secular* opinion—with a sharper edge. In short, the polarization of public debate on most issues is simply aided and abetted by the polarization of the religious forces. There is little "othering" yet reconciling and healing dialogue. Our particular points are too important for that. Few would really want a major effort to be put forward to see whether there are not better ways to be or try to be the church speaking. That might threaten some cherished particular policy we most urgently want to be sure is spoken to the church and to the world. So we say that these others have "dropped out of the dialogue."

4. The statement that was adopted on nuclear war[25] should be considered along with the addresses on peace in a nuclear age that were given at the conference. Nuclear war is condemned in the strongest possible moral and religious terms. The relevant paragraphs are:

94. The development of military technology, and especially of atomic, radiological, biological and chemical arms and the means to deliver them, marks a decisive turning point in the history of mankind, of states and their wars. The frightful possibilities of indiscriminate war exterminating not only combatants but civilian populations as well, the impossibility of self-defense by smaller nations, the danger of annihilation of human cultures, the continuing danger for future generations from radiation—all this radically changes the situation of the states and their relations with one another.

95. This new and terrible situation forces Christians to re-examine previous thinking in the churches concerning war and the function of the state in relation to it. In Amsterdam in 1948, the First Assembly of the WCC declared, "War is contrary to the will of God." At the same time it acknowledged three attitudes towards the participation by Christians in the evil of war, one of the three attitudes being that war might at times be a lesser evil. Today the situation has changed. Christians still differ as to whether military means can be legitimately used to achieve objectives which are necessary to justice. But nuclear war goes beyond all bounds. Mutual nuclear annihilation can never establish justice because it destroys all that justice seeks to defend or to achieve. We now say to all governments and peoples that nuclear war is against God's will and the greatest of evils. Therefore we affirm that it is the first duty of governments and their officials to prevent nuclear war.

In this statement the governing consideration is what was meant by "nuclear war." What was meant is nuclear war that "goes beyond all bounds." It is "mutual nuclear annihilation" which, of course, "can never establish justice because it destroys all that justice seeks to defend or to achieve." "We now say to all governments and peoples that nuclear war is against God's will and the greatest of evils. Therefore we affirm that it is the first duty of governments and their officials to prevent nuclear war." On this understanding of the nature of nuclear war, i.e., given the level and unlimitedness of nuclear war that was in mind, this is indubitably correct.

But this, it must be pointed out, was not to push very far into the nuclear problem or the responsibility of governments in the use of power for peace and justice in a nuclear age. It might equally well have been said that, because of the fundamental change brought about by nuclear weapons, the nation-state system is contrary to the will of God, and that the first duty of governments and their officials is to abolish it. Both the prevention of nuclear war and the supplanting of the nation-state system are rational requirements in the nuclear age; or rather, these are different statements of the same requirement. In either case, one has a whole range of problems and political obligations to analyze that involve living under and "using" what was just resoundingly declared to be contrary to God's will. In either case, a seemingly precise directive is only but definitely a direction. In thus correctly prophesying against indiscriminate war exterminating practically all mankind, the report may be read by many as a sweeping condemnation of any and all use of any nuclear weapons in any war or for deterrence; and *that* would be impossible and morally wrong to say to Christians or citizens of any of the great powers in the nuclear age. I am not sure this was understood at Geneva, or analyzed adequately, as we went about eschewing other people's use of armed force. Which is to

103

say, the connection between force and policy is still as strong as it ever was; and will remain so until the nation-state is put under.

Likewise, if the direction pointed out as the government's first duty had been by saying the nation-state system is contrary to the will of God, because the nation can no longer defend what one wants to defend or achieve what one wants to achieve, that would not have been very helpful if understood as a specific directive. I am not sure this was thoroughly understood at Geneva either. There was a good deal of Kellogg-Briand mentality, which came out, for example, in the statement that "all agree on the goal of the rejection of military activity by sovereign states" [26]—whatever *that* may mean. The nation was seen to be important when one hadn't got it; at the same time there were signs of a return to the time when Reinhold Niebuhr apparently accepted the use of force in class struggle but believed the use of force between national collectives or to preserve justice politically embodied in an established national entity no longer justified. Still these are small matters in the report on international relations, which throughout wrestles with the structural problem of how peace, justice, and order can be secured in a pluralistic world. I mention them, and the very great strengths of the report, only to show by analogy with something else that could have been condemned in the same strong terms, that there remain structural problems in the very analysis of the political use of violence that are only covered over when it is said that "nuclear war is against God's will" (par. 95).

This expression was used in order to build upon the statement of the First Assembly of the WCC in Amsterdam in 1948, which declared, "War is contrary to the will of God." Although that would seem to settle the matter, the assembly went on to say that there are still three attitudes toward doing this "evil" which is "contrary to the will of God." The 1966 Geneva statement imputes to itself a connection with the 1948 Assembly statement by adding (incorrectly, I judge) concerning Amsterdam: "one of the three attitudes being that war might at times be a lesser evil." [27] This is no longer the case, the present statement affirms, with regard to nuclear war when its effects are as the report describes them. The contrary is true: Nuclear war is the greatest of evils; nuclear war is against God's will.

Now, I suppose there must have been some theologians and ethicists (*"periti"*) who between the 1948 Assembly at Amsterdam and Geneva 1966 have subjected to devastating criticism these astonishing assertions (or at least the terminology) about great groups of Christians believing it to be right for them to do something that is evil, a sin, unjust, and, indeed, contrary to the will of God. If there were not such *periti* serving the councils of the churches in this way, there should have been. If there were, then there must be some way found to integrate the work of *periti* into the writing of conference documents without making them Council Fathers. Amsterdam should not have been quoted by rote or for precedent in order to compose a set of questionable propositions.[28]

This is as if it were said: *War is unthinkable.* Christians, however, fall into three groups. Some say that this unthinkable thing ought never to be done. Others that it may be done if done *justly* or in defense of the rule of law.[29] Still others hold the view that war might at times be the lesser evil. But *nuclear* war has changed all that. Nuclear war would be the greatest evil. Therefore we affirm that *nuclear war is unthinkable* and that the first duty of government is to prevent it.

Now if one is going to begin by taking the first, strange step of saying flatly that war is contrary to the will of God but that Christians legitimately differ in the attitudes they take toward engaging in it, then one might not have chosen to proceed through the option which says that war might at times be a lesser evil, coming thus with such compelling logic to the conclusion that since the times have changed, nuclear war is the greatest of evils and contrary to God's will (which "contrary" seems now to have a force in universally prohibiting specific action that the first "contrary" never had). Instead, one can choose to proceed through another option, and say that while war is contrary to the perfect will of God, Christians may and do act on the belief that they should participate in war if it is *just*. That too would be a conclusion passing strange, but it is an available one if one is going to proceed without a radical reform of doctrine from Oxford and Amsterdam. Still, it would have enabled and required deliberations in 1966 to press deeper into the moral dimension of the problem of war in a nuclear age and into a number of things that still have to be said about the possession and use of nuclear weapons (apart from the statement, which is true enough, that the *kind* of nuclear war the drafters of the Geneva report apparently had in mind would be the greatest of evils).

As it stands, this conclusion is only apparently a particular, specific verdict. Instead, it can be formulated as a general principle to read (copying the language of the Second Vatican Council) : "Any act of war which in destructiveness goes beyond all bounds, amounts to mutual nuclear suicide, and destroys all that one wants to defend or to achieve is a crime against God and man himself. It merits unequivocal and unhesitating condemnation." Or one can as well say this in the language used at Geneva, noting the *general terms* characterizing the *kind* of war that we have seen was condemned (that is, noting the restrictive clause "which . . .") : "We now say to all governments and peoples that nuclear war which in destructiveness goes beyond all bounds, amounts to mutual nuclear suicide, and destroys all one wants to defend or to achieve is against God's will and the greatest of evils. Therefore we affirm that it is the first duty of governments and their officials to prevent such nuclear war." This states the *principle of proportion* governing the political use of force, whereas the fathers of the Vatican Council chose instead the *principle of discrimination* as the central judgment to be addressed to the governments and peoples of the world: "Any act of war aimed indiscriminately at the destruction of entire cities or of extensive areas along with their population is a crime against God and man himself. It merits unequivocal and unhesitating condemnation." [30] *Both* of these action- and policy-relevant principles governing the political use of armed force are clearly present in each of these documents, of course; only the Geneva Conference stressed one of them while the Vatican Council stressed the other. Each of these statements is an *ethical* judgment expressed properly in *moral* terms which are *general* ones. They use, philosophers would say, "moral-*species*-terms" to describe the *kind* of action or war we are talking about, and offense terms to condemn them. As such, neither of these judgments seeks to supplant the office of political prudence in making particular judgments of fact or application.

This is the way the statement on nuclear war adopted at Geneva can and may and must be understood, but not likely the way in which it will be understood, nor likely the prevailing understanding of it at the conference. It is of the very nature of the Church and Society Syndrome to believe that there is such a thing as hybrid or satyrlike statements of *moral fact* within the scope of prophecy and precise preaching, and within the competence of Christian deliberation as such, or the deliberations of Christians as such. Statements of moral fact would melt together moral judgments and fact verdicts, principle and application, into something else that is somehow neither and both. The older way of doing this was not to have any reserve about moving from the action- and policy-revelant statements ecumenial ethics can and should be making all the time in discussing social ethics and the nature of a responsible society to quite particular recommendations and incriminations. The newer "orthodox" way of doing this is to suppose that the Christian life is composed of the insights which come as a man stands with the Bible in one hand and the facts in the other responding to what God is doing in the world in Christ's ever coming lordship over the powers. In either case the office of political prudence would be supplanted or usurped.

Therefore, the formulation adopted at Geneva that "nuclear war is against God's will and the greatest of evils" is apt to be taken as a statement of *moral fact,* and moreover one that condemns much more than it does. I have said that this is, in my opinion, indubitably correct as an ethical statement of one of the principles governing the responsible political use of violence and also that it is the application to be made to the factual situation which those who wrote it apprehended to be the case, had in mind, and characterized as they did.

What is at stake in keeping statements of ethico-political principle separate and distinct from their specific application is the integrity of the office of political prudence, and the right of persons in their official capacities of magistrate or citizen not to have their consciences faulted, their freedom in the slightest degree overborne, if they disagree. What is at stake is that persons in the political and military sectors of our society ought not to have their final weighty responsibility in the exercise of political prudence in the slightest degree eased when it happens that they agree with one of these particular judgments of moral fact issued by church councils or conferences of churchmen sponsored by the churches. What is at stake is also, and far more importantly, the integrity of and our unswerving attention to the fullness and adequacy of our articulation of judgments oriented upon public policy in ecumenical Christian social ethics. Taken as a specific statement of moral fact, it seems that the Geneva pronouncement rests directly upon some analytic circularity in summary of the facts, like "Nuclear war going beyond all bounds goes beyond all bounds," or "Nuclear war destroying all that one wants to defend destroys all that one wants to defend"—for which the only statable reason for condemning any such thing would be some ultimate like "Love life" or "God's will." Understood in this way, the Geneva pronouncement ignores its own foundation in a statable prior principle that makes sense and is illuminating and fecund for much else besides (namely, the principle of proportion) ; if this had not been suppressed, it would also have been evident that more such statable principles are needed.

We need to attend first of all not to the business of getting moral facts but to the business of Christian reflection upon all sorts and structures of human activity. Then we will know that there is a describable kind of barely humanly tolerable human activity known as "war" that sometimes is necessary and justifiable.[31] We would know that Christian ethics must be able to say and say very clearly a number of kinds of things about this; we would be enabled and required to say much more than at Geneva we were impelled or able to say in adopting a conclusion that no one would have to be a Christian or go to Geneva or have his political conscience instructed from Geneva in order to know.[32] At the same time, the resulting formulation would

109

not have been such that it permits anyone, and permitted very many of those who adopted it, to suppose the statement condemns or entails an ethical condemnation of any conceivable use of any and all nuclear weapons in any possible war and/or their use for deterrence. That would be something, as we shall see, that none of our fellow Christians from around the world should have said to the Christians in the United States or to our government, something no Christian should have contributed to or have brought back with him as a finding of the conference if he could have helped it, and something no one should use to inform his conscience.

It seems incredible that the planning committee would have supposed that conference addresses by a couple of Middle Europeans and a Japanese would provide adequate consideration of Christian responsibility for "Peace in a Nuclear Age," with no one to speak from the point of view of the church in the world's five nuclear powers. This was not the way to find out what Mr. M. M. Thomas, cochairman of the conference, seemed to assert in his final address had happened in those two weeks, namely, an answer to the question whether the ecumenical movement "can stand a real understanding," can endure if every group is "a disturbing element to some other."

Yoshiaki Iisaka punctured a number of things he regarded as nuclear "illusions," and finally as a "way out" spoke of "peace teams." There was a good deal to be said for the modesty of his understanding of the fruit to be expected from such teams, for the advancement of the *koinonia* and the creation of an international ethos and a political "witness," in comparison with the goal stated in the final report of accumulating a steadily increasing storehouse of facts and information enabling the world church to be able to deal with particular problems of world peace even more competently, or in comparison with the rather self-lacerating expectation of some of the Americans that from this we would learn the way to world peace.

Max Kohnstamm of Holland gave the address that was most informed by Christian realism concerning political action in general, and with some elements of this we will deal later; but he did not directly address the special problem of Christian morality and nuclear weaponry.

This brings us to Helmut Gollwitzer, professor of theology in West Berlin. His nuclear pacifist position was the sole positive *analysis* heard by the conference, since there were simply three rather emotional speeches, no real discussion, that followed from the floor.[33] Gollwitzer's call was for a personal commitment on the part of all Christians, for them to say an absolute No to nuclear weapons. He acknowledged that until now the two main positions on participation in war have both been appropriate, and each supplemented the other:

The answer given by Christian pacifism leaves to non-Christians that very secular task which requires the greatest love and unselfishness, namely the use of force; and the answer given by the great churches involves Christians so deeply in the conflicts of the world and in the settlement of these conflicts by the use of lethal force that it is almost impossible for Christians to bear witness to the joyful message of Christ to their adversaries.

Nuclear weapons create a radically new situation only for those who support this second answer; and the question now raised by nuclear weapons for Christian conscience can be answered only one way.

Gollwitzer pointed out, i.e., he *asserted,* that the tests of justice in war are all no longer valid, and he affirmed that "on this there is general agreement"—all this without any

111

close argument of the point and without, it must be said, a correct understanding of the meaning of discrimination in acts of war. Albeit, the just war theory had sufficient life left in it to condemn, in a parenthesis, the American intervention in Vietnam just before its demise.

It may also be of some interest that, asserting the just war tests to "bear the stamp of a feudal age," Professor Gollwitzer addressed himself to the question of revolution in Christian ethics today and specifically to Professor Schaull's call for us to start *de novo* and develop criteria for revolutionary action. These old ideas of justice in war, Gollwitzer asserted, made "no distinction between the rebellion of a medieval aristocrat against his feudal lord and the modern revolution of suppressed people." It again is not applicable, and we must pay attention to Lenin's rejection of the doctrine of the just war and to how the struggle of the people against oppression is justified.

The just war theory bears instead the stamp of the paramount question for Christian conscience of how in any struggle one is still going to speak for man—all men; and the limits upon war that exhibit the fact that one is going still to be controlled by awesome respect for the image of God in man, for the sacredness in the historical order who is man. These limits still prevailed in the doctrine of justifiable revolution that was developed in Calvinism; this did not depend on any feudal notions of aristocratic rebellion. But that, of course, spoke of man, freedom, rights, and for moderation and compromise. It was indeed the spirit abroad among many at the conference simply to justify the struggle of the oppressed without confronting the question of criteria of justice and without having other limits upon revolution than the end in view. This was to proceed in the search for tests as if we had none.

In any case, in Gollwitzer's view, Christians must so "unanimously and unconditionally" say No to nuclear war that this brings everything nuclear indiscriminately under condemnation. "Whoever has recourse to atomic warfare . . . will have God against him. No government and no individual must make use of this menace [what does this mean for the question of deterrence to which we will come in a moment?], no one must participate in its use. At any rate we Christians . . . refuse to participate . . . for we can only do what can be done in the name of Jesus Christ." This is certainly a position to which many may resort under the anguish of the nuclear dilemma.

However, Professor Gollwitzer did not see the consequence of this for the Christian church in that it must then become completely a sect in regard to the modern state— selectively no doubt, but not at all selectively in regard to nuclear weapons or in regard to the deterrent state. Instead of saying this forthrightly, he pictured the churches urging their governments "to regard possession of these weapons as a mandate entrusted to them by the international community of nations"; and many another proposition having to do with "cooperating with politicians in finding a way out"—even though the Christian has already, presumably, found his way out by renouncing any use of nuclear weapons and even though, presumably, no Christian could be a politician.

In a compact phrase, Gollwitzer thought of the absolute commitment he called for as the first task, and doing something about the peace based on a precarious balance of deterrence as the second task—both Christian tasks, not contradictions: "It is only when the church undertakes the first of these tasks that the second task becomes urgent," he said. "And it is only if the church undertakes the second of these tasks that its rejection of the use of weapons of

113

mass destruction will be more than an empty phrase, a comfortable ethical attitude which involves no concrete responsibility." Here still speaks the tradition of the great churches, although in the first place it had been affirmed that, with regard to these modern weapons of war, that tradition was no longer applicable.

I should say, rather, that if the church undertakes to say this No unanimously and unconditionally, the problem of deterrence will not then become urgent. Instead there will immediately be no more problem of deterrence as at all a problem for Christians. And if politicians with whom we might be still wanting to cooperate in finding a way out really listened to the church, there would immediately be no deterrence and therefore no urgent problem for them; and no moral problem remaining in regard to it for Christians or for politicians, not for one moment after governments came to believe what Gollwitzer wants the church to say in the first place.[34]

The *actuality* of deterrence depends upon a credible belief, mutually shared, that one might *use* a nuclear weapon. If the government of one of the great powers were persuaded by the churches never to be willing to use any nuclear weapon under any circumstances, and this were known, there would instantly be no deterrence and therefore no practical problem of finding a way out. Likewise, the *morality* of deterrence depends upon it not being wholly immoral for a government ever to use an atomic weapon under any circumstances. If those who use any nuclears in any way in any war will have God against them, God is against the possession of all these weapons right now for deterrence. It would be inexcusable even to be ambiguous about it, or ambiguous about the use to be made of dual-purpose weapons (upon legitimate military targets or upon cities), or to temporize in dismantling deterrence or to de-

114

lay resigning from office or withdrawing from helpfully cooperating with politicians, if no use of any nuclear weapon could ever possibly be justified.

This is the case with regard to anything said to be inherently immoral. To remain conditionally willing or to threaten or to seem to be ready to do an immoral act is of a piece with the immorality of that act itself. No one ever said that an act of adultery is not an evil in addition to the adulterous thought, but we have it on rather high authority that the adulterous thought partakes of the same intrinsic wrong that it may lead to. So with acts of war using a nuclear weapon. If that would be in itself always under any circumstances and in any manner, an evil thing to do to which we must unconditionally say No (let us say, because this would be an act of murder), then threatening to do so would be the same *sort* of evil (though not the same evil), and deterrence rests upon murderous thinking, and this would not for one moment be justifiable. One could not too quickly resign from office after accepting Gollwitzer's verdict; there would be no second task, and no more cooperating with politicians for Christians to undertake. The only thing remaining to be said would be that the "peace of a sort" which deterrence maintains for the peoples of the world among whom Christians dwell makes our peace also a guilty peace.

The foregoing has had one purpose only: to point out again, as was done in connection with the Geneva statement on nuclear war, the crucial issues that remain even to be formulated in ecumenical social ethics in dealing with questions of war and peace in the nuclear age. If the statement on nuclear war was meant to say what Gollwitzer said or is understood to say this; if that were the conclusion Christians addressed to the world, in saying so flatly that "nuclear war is against God's will" (and I believe

115

that it was not), then these issues simply cannot arise as problems for Christians, nor could we have any standing to proffer guidance upon them, or upon many another problem of war and peace in the present age to which we continue to speak. On the other hand, if the statement on nuclear war had not been so seemingly particular and lacking in discrimination concerning the kind of thing that was meant to be condemned, then these issues would have opened up.

One word only about Kohnstamm's address as this may be related to the responsibilities of Christians in a country like ours. He called his speech "God's Command and the Change of Social Structures"; I would call it "The Structural Ingredient of Responsible Political Action in the Nation-State System"—not having particularly to do with the "nuclear age." We face, he said, a vicious circle: "Peace and community between nations are impossible without binding and protective law; binding and protecting law is impossible without community." Christians have yet to learn the lesson about international relations they learned about domestic society; namely, that "love passes not directly from man to man, but through structures." There is no solution but to look inside the existing structures for cracks where a change might take place (Roger Mehl).

In doing this we have in mind that there is no man, and certainly no collectivity, in which Cain exists no longer. But the important point Kohnstamm made was that structures serve to protect against the unpredictabilities of the other collectivities, not especially or not only against their evilness. The international order has in it such defects that there is only force to safeguard against the other collective's unpredictability. The nation-state is surrounded by arbitrariness on all sides; the other is always a potential enemy, etc., where there are no dependable structures through which identification may pass. The considerable strengths of the report on international relations that came out of Geneva was the degree to which its analysis was pointed in this direction by Kohnstamm, John Bennett, and doubtless others of similar views.

This seems to me an important point to stress for Christians in America for the maturity and understanding we may need to have in all that we think and say about the responsibilities of public office. It cannot simply be said that the "cold war" is over and there are now opportunities for reconciliation. The question rather is whether or not there are cracks where a change in international structures can be initiated and take root. It is not that state and defense prepare always for the worst, when they should have a better picture of the world. It is rather that the responsibilities of public office is to prepare for the unpredictabilities. Within that we can debate endlessly about the internal changes going on in some communist countries, or the difference between a pluralism of national communisms and Stalinism or between Russia and China today; about converging economic interests, and how far communist aggressiveness has abated and to what degree continued frustration of another nation's purposes may be needed in the pedagogy by which those purposes may be moderated and become reconcilable with the interests of others, etc. Still it is the case that a government official has responsibility for the nation in face of the unpredictabilities. He cannot and should not risk national security,[35] even though he may seek to make national interests coincide with the interests of others, and he too should look inside the structures to see where new structures may be possible along which identification will pass. Still the nation-state system is in a *state* of war. That had better not be denied in the course of saying that even a state of war is not without moral limits govern-

117

ing it, and in the course of charting the direction in which that system may be changed.

A PROVISIONAL MODEL
FOR SPECIFIC
POLITICAL PRONOUNCEMENTS

I propose to introduce here a preliminary model for what may be an improvement in the methodology of ecumenical pronouncements on political and social questions before going on, in the final section of this paper, to ask whether Vatican Council II may not offer a better example from which to learn.

This is only a provisional model. It can, I believe, be improved upon. Still this would be one way of forcing ourselves to formulate particularistic recommendations more responsibly, if these are going to continue to be made. It would require of us more realistic thinking concerning the hard options that may face persons in leadership in the economic, political, and military sectors of our society. If we are not going to place upon ourselves a self-denying ordinance that holds us back from specifying the decisions that fall within the office of political prudence, then at least we need to impose upon ourselves a way of speaking about particular courses of action which seem desirable that takes account of the costs these actions may entail and makes explicit the hard choice that may (for all our hopes) be the only alternative. Christians, meeting as such, should not allow themselves to advocate particular policies in the public forum without also specifying how we are to get from where we are. We ought not to allow ourselves to specify only the optimistic among the prospects if certain steps are taken without specifying also that to take these steps may entail that other steps be taken that are rather grim, even if possibly less grim than where we are.

To make clear that this is so is the purpose of my provisional model of how specific pronouncements might responsibly be made. This suggestion is, therefore, a hypothesis in two senses. It is a hypothesis contrary to the fact, i.e., contrary to the way in which too often we Christians presently address the world. It is also a hypothesis contrary to what I believe to be more desirable, for which we shall have to search in better models.

The purpose of the address of the church to the world, or of church sponsored congresses addressing the public, ought to be the broadening and deepening of public debate on urgent questions; it ought not to be to stop or narrow down this debate or polarize the debate that is going on by a finding in favor of a specific policy behind which we are seeking merely to mobilize opinion. At the same time, statements made with a view to opening a larger consideration of issues and possible particular actions ought not even to be formulated so as to leave the impression that Christians as such have insights that would supplant the office of political judgment and decision on the part of magistrate and citizens, bind or fault their consciences, or in the slightest degree ease their special responsibility for deciding in regard to matters beyond anything their faith or the churches can tell them.

With these premises in mind, there is something to be said in favor of the statement of the Archbishop of Canter-

119

bury on British action in regard to Rhodesia. He was under considerable pressure to say to the government that military force should be used against the Ian Smith regime and in behalf of multiracial guarantees before the independence of that country should be recognized. That would have been to take a stand on both the ends Great Britain should serve and the means as well; and it would have intervened on matters on which Christians may have legitimate disagreement. Instead he said: *If the Prime Minister finds it necessary to use force, the government will not fail to have support from Christian opinion.*

It is not for us as Christian churches to give the Government military advice as to what is practical or possible. That is not our function. . . . If [the Prime Minister] and his Government think it necessary to use force for the perpetuation of our existing obligations in Rhodesia, then a great body of Christian opinion in this country would support him in so doing. I do not think it would be right for us to say less than that.[1]

This is worth considering as a model, even if it does bring to mind an image of British soldiers refusing to fire on white Rhodesians and the Prime Minister calling up the Christian forces! It had the virtue of urging upon the government the possible costs as well as the high priority to be placed upon the cause of justice: if in order to secure greater justice in the constitution of Rhodesia the Prime Minister finds it necessary to use armed force, he will not find himself forsaken by Christian opinion.

A final virtue of adopting this as the grammar of Christian address to the world's problems, in place of the grammar of dissent or particular partisanship, is that this formula can be used in a way that will force churchmen themselves to weigh the alternatives more responsibly. In thus attempting to contribute to a greater openness in public debate, churchmen might at the same time contribute to this very pondering of options in the public domain. If the churches and churchmen as such are going to issue statements that make particular recommendations or indicate quite specifically the direction in which they believe public policy should go, this is perhaps a way of doing this with a greater degree of self-imposed responsibility and of inducing more responsible deliberations among ourselves and in the public domain.

In conclusion, a few examples may be fashioned to stimulate thought upon this question:

1. If the Administration, in order to stop the bombing of targets in North Vietnam and the destruction in the South, and in order for civic action programs to go forward, should find it necessary to fight a longer war against the Viet Cong, the United States government will not find itself forsaken by Christian opinion.[2]

2. If the Administration in order to bring peace in Vietnam and to accept a "national communism" for that whole country as a lesser evil than the destruction entailed in trying longer to prevent its *imposition* should find it necessary to prepare for and/or make known the strongest possible United States guarantees of conventional and nuclear protection against subversive or conventional attacks upon the Philippines,[3] Japan, Taiwan, Australia, Indonesia, Malaysia, Thailand,[4] *or* India,[5] the President will not find himself forsaken by Christian opinion.

3. If in order to extricate ourselves from South Vietnam the Administration should find it necessary to establish, clearly and for all to see, other forms or loci of American military presence in Asia, the President would not fail to find support in a large body of Christian opinion in this country.[6]

4. If in order to secure an international treaty pledging

121

"no *first* use of nuclear weapons" the Administration should find it necessary to increase greatly the standing army and other conventional forces and to call for a shelter program to protect a portion of the population comparable to that of Sweden, the government would not fail to be supported by Christian opinion.

5. If in order to secure an international treaty pledging *"no* use of nuclear weapons" the Administration found it necessary to go to universal service in the armed forces and otherwise greatly to strengthen conventional defense, the government would not be forsaken by Christian opinion in this country.[7]

6. If, in response to the Soviet deployment of an anti-missile system, and in order to avoid magnifying and improving our counter-society offensive weapons, or to avoid meaning to use them, the Administration should find it necessary to deploy a defensive antimissile system (and correlated with this a system of fallout shelters), the President will not fail to be supported by a large body of Christian opinion in this country. (This proposition can be reversed, to *oppose* United States deployment of an antimissile system, indicating what we are willing to say about the wisdom and morality of putting greater weight on our deterrence of nuclear war by the sort of weapon it would be immoral ever to use as apparently intended, and increasingly necessary that we intend to use them.)

7. If in order to extend a credible nuclear protection to countries in Asia that in the future may need and desire this against a Chinese nuclear threat, and to avoid a too extensive American military presence in that area of the world, the Administration should find an antimissile system to be requisite,[8] the President will not fail to be supported by a large body of Christian opinion in this country.

These are a few examples in the area of national defense

policy. It is not assumed that other sorts of policy are not more important in looking inside the structures to find the point and the time for new procedures to take root. It is only assumed that a nation, and especially a nation that has inherited great power and great responsibilities, must consider the alternatives proposed to it not in an ideal light but in face of the unpredictabilities in the action of other great and dynamic collectives. To forget this is a mistake Christians sometimes make while putting forward particular recommendations to government. The foregoing formulations of some possible, still rather specific pronouncements are designed to jog our memories, and the memories of our fellow citizens among whom these interventions might be made; and to call attention to alternatives that we need to know are not grimmer if we mean to try to influence public policy in any such definite ways.

One could continue in the same vein and frame a couple of alternatives that are more political than military in character:

8. If in order to "normalize" our relations as a Pacific power with mainland China the President should find it necessary to dampen down the pressures and the momentum toward, as a world power, our détente with the Soviet Union or, as an Atlantic power, toward a united Europe, he would find broad support in Christian opinion. (Or *vice versa*.)

9. If in order to attain universal membership in the United Nations (by the admission of Red China) the President should find it necessary to accept the fact that fewer world problems could be mediated or resolved by action through the United Nations, and that, for a decade or more, more (not less) reliance would have to be placed on *unilateral* national initiatives, some likely involving resort to the use of armed force, the President would nevertheless not be forsaken by Christian opinion in this country.

123

The present writer would not want conferences of churchmen, meeting as such, to say these things, even though I believe these are fair statements of the alternatives our political leaders may face. This would, however, be one way to place upon ourselves the necessity of responsibly thinking through the alternatives we believe that Christians ought to be willing to support if we are going to continue to tell statesmen and citizens the precise policies that cannot be justified and which therefore should be opposed. It would be better to seek the ways and the self-denying ordinances that will insure that such conferences, whether representative or not, do all that it is humanly possible to do in order for them to become more like the church speaking.

TOWARD AN
ECUMENICAL ETHICS

In this it may be helpful for all of us to take a good look at the newer half of the ecumenical movement, at the social encyclicals of John XXIII, at the addresses of Paul VI, and especially at the "Pastoral Constitution on the Church in the Modern World" issued by Vatican Council II. In no sense can it be said of these documents that in speaking to the world the church tried to be anything other than the church speaking, or that choice was made between politically irrelevant generalities and speaking beyond the competence of the church too particularly. This, of course, was because these documents and their source were in structural ways appointed to speak for the church. The older ecumenical movement is not so organized, and cannot be at any time in the foreseeable future. Its conferences speak only for themselves, and the central boards of the NCC and the WCC do not as such speak for their member denominations. Still nothing prevents our taking as a model the substantive reserve of the Vatican Council in addressing the world, its concentration on speaking in Christian terms when doing so, and possibly some of its procedures, to see what may be learned from these things. It is what we mean and intend to do by Christian address to the world, and not the pluralistic organization of the older ecumenical movement, that is the chief problem. This can be seen from the fact that a single Protestant denomination speaking for itself to urgent public questions very often uses this same particularistic style which the Vatican Council, for example, did not presume to adopt.

When John XXIII made his "opening to the left," he struck down a programmatic anticommunism within church circles that was helping to render political decisions inflexible. But he did not presume, upon the moral authority of his religious leadership, to put in its place a program of immediate reconciliation with some or any of the brands of more liberal national communism. He endorsed no *unilinear* theory of the development of diversity or domestic liberality in the communist movement. He claimed no prescience about the actual possibilities of political accommodation at any particular time.

In order not to do any of these things, he had expressly to disavow any such intention while drawing attention to these possible developments. From everything stated in *Pacem in terris* about human rights, the exigencies of human nature and historical movements, Pope John simply drew the conclusion that "it can happen" that "meetings"

125

are actually useful. This entails that it can at times happen that they are not, and that issues fail to be resolved by negotiation. "To decide whether this moment has arrived . . . these are problems that can only be solved with the virtue of prudence." Whether a moment for fruitful negotiation (which should always be held open as a possible occurrence and as an opportunity we seek) has actually arrived is a decision, the encyclical expressly states, which "rests primarily with those who live and work in the specific sectors of human society in which these problems arise" (par. 160).

This seems to me to be a model of the church speaking relevantly to the world without ceasing to be the *church* speaking. Its merit is not only that it avoids becoming an exercise in specific policy making. The merit is also that by taking care *not* to speak too specifically to the world the church was not led astray from its primary task of speaking the whole of the Christian understanding of man's political existence. Thus *Pacem in terris* never concentrated so much on urgent particular problems that, while addressing them, it failed to elaborate a doctrine of moral law and justice and human rights, on which the Johannine teaching rests. By remembering to speak for the church, it spoke more fully for man, and it addressed nothing to men of goodwill everywhere or to political leaders that could not be believed to be drawn from charity as the heart and soul of social justice. Where disagreement about how to accomplish these things legitimately arises, the church did not presume to speak.

In contrast, many current Protestant "openings to the left" are so excessively anxious to bring peace to a torn world and to say precisely what men in the leadership of the political sector of our societies ought to do in order to foster revolutionary social reconstruction that they fail to speak for the church, for the entirety of Christian political insights, and they speak not nearly so well for man and his liberty or for political order based on truth and justice. Too much is made too quickly of the "freedom and diversity" appearing in the communist world, without asking whether *that* is what the church today, or any churchman, should mean by human liberty. What God is doing in something called "revolution" becomes the focus of attention, and because God's command is seen to be narrowly here there is insufficient witness to the need for freedom and just order. There is an inadequate input into ecumenical ethics because we are too much concerned that the church speak very particularly to men in a revolutionary age and do not remember that even on that it should be the church speaking.[1]

When Pope Paul recommended that the conflict in Vietnam be brought before the UN, he put this idea forward most tentatively. It was almost a prayer. "Who knows," he said, "if finally an arbitration of the United Nations, confided to the neutral nations, might tomorrow—we would like to hope even today—resolve this terrible question. Let us pray to God for this." And while presuming to offer this specific suggestion, he was careful to note that "judgment of political questions and temporal interests" are outside his competence as a religious leader and spokesman. He also took the trouble to distinguish on this occasion his own long record of appeals for peace from "pacifism, which ignores relative rights and duties in the conflict in question," with which political leaders must be concerned.[2]

One looks in vain for a similar degree of reserve in a number of non-Roman pronouncements upon political questions, or for equal care when addressing public questions to distinguish between the competences of men in the church or when speaking as churchmen and the competence and the task of people with their leaders in the realm of the state. This is strange today when in every respect other

127

than social ethics and political policy it is supposed on all sides that the pan-Protestant era, indeed the Christian era, is ended. It is passing strange that we Protestants have a passion for particular pronouncements that might have been appropriate in pan-Protestantism, and in our ecumenical movement the same syndrome which might have been appropriate in "Christendom." Yet the fact is that Roman Catholicism, which has its roots in medievalism, seems today in a pluralistic society better able to distinguish the church herself from the state, and seems to have a greater respect for the integrity of the public realm and for the office of political prudence.

It is a sorry commentary upon these times and upon Christianity today that people and clergy alike seem not to know the difference between two sorts of competence, between the moral and political insights that may come from the heart of the Christian faith and the competence we all may have, in varying degrees, to make the decisions that belong to the exercise of political prudence. Even if Pope Paul's actual capacities make him Everyman's candidate for Premier of the World, his reservation about not having directly and specifically to do with temporal political affairs was correct. Protestantism, especially, has today conjoined assertedly momentary prophetic response to God's will and action with concrete political decision making, to the confusion of all distinctions concerning what can and what cannot be said in Christ's name. This is a confusion of terms and of competencies that has replaced (of all things, in a religiously "pluralistic" society) the various mixtures of "church" and "state" that formerly prevailed. Amazingly, the Catholic Church and Catholic churchmen seem more aware of the need for avoiding this confusion when the church or Christians speak to the world—*"especially* in pluralistic societies" (76)[3]—than does the older ecumenical movement in its social ethics.[4]

We should take most seriously the "Pastoral Constitution on the Church in the Modern World" as a measure of *how* the church should attempt to speak both for the church and to every urgent social and political problem today. Notable in the first place is the fact that the text (Part II) that is addressed to "Some Problems of Special Urgency" (numbered paragraphs 46-93, or approximately 60 pages) is preceded by paragraphs 1-45 comprising 49 pages, in which is set forth the church's understanding of the dignity of the human person, the common good, the norms applicable to political community, etc., as these are to be seen in the light of Christ. This compares favorably with the brief theological-ethical prefaces that ordinarily precede the specific comments addressed to particular problems in documents from the older ecumenical movement.[5] In fact, I should say, the fine work of relevantly refining the principles of Christian social ethics in Part I and the fact that Part II *stops short of specificity* in the analysis of particular problems and in stating the directions in which solutions to them may be found—*these are functions of one another.* If the former is truly achieved, the church or spokesmen for the church will discover that they cannot on that authority, reach particular recommendations.

The Vatican Council set itself the task of explaining to everyone how it conceives of "the presence and activity of the Church in the world today" (2) ; it did not first of all set itself problem-solving exercises, however urgently these might be needed. It wanted only *"in the light of Christ . . .* to speak to all men in order to illuminate the mystery of man and to *cooperate* in finding the solution to the outstanding problems of our time" (10), to speak of the church's "healing and elevating impact on the dignity of the person"

(40), to lead and guide Christians and enlighten all mankind, "as they *search for answers* to questions of such complexity" (46, introducing Part II), to *"direct* the mind to solutions which are fully human" (11), to show that, whatever the problem, there can be no solution to it unless the social order "be founded on truth, built on justice and animated by love; in freedom it should grow every day towards a more humane balance" (26), and to speak as church the meaning of this to the world today.

This meant that anything specifically said had to begin with the express acknowledgment that the church or Christian ethics does not always have "at hand the solution to particular problems" (33) and that whoever proposes a particular solution does so beyond the competence of the church speaking. The traditional claim is made, of course, that the church "has the right to pass moral judgments, even on matters touching the political order"; but the basis and the limits of this claim over "mixed areas" are kept very clear: "whenever basic personal rights or the salvation of souls make such judgments necessary" (76).[6]

The accent, then, properly falls on "The Help Which the Church Strives to Give to Human Activity through Christians" (section title before par. 43).; and it is they who must arrive at solutions. This means, on the one hand, that the faithful will know, as the council did not forget, that "no better way exists for attaining a truly human political life than by fostering an inner sense of justice, benevolence, and service for the common good, and by strengthening basic beliefs about the true nature of the political community, and about the proper exercise and limits of public authority" (73). It means, on the other hand, that "the faithful will be able to make a clear distinction between what a Christian conscience leads them to do in their own name as citizens, whether as individuals or in

130

association, and what they do in the name of the Church and in union with her shepherds" (76).

Laymen should . . . know that it is generally the function of their well-formed Christian conscience to see that the divine law is inscribed in the life of the earthly city. . . . Let the layman not imagine that his pastors are always such experts, that to every problem which arises, however complicated, they can readily give him a concrete solution, *or even that such is their mission.* . . .
Often enough the Christian view of things will itself suggest some specific solution in certain circumstances. Yet it happens rather frequently, *and legitimately so,* that with equal sincerity some of the faithful will disagree with others on a given matter. Even against the intentions of their proponents, however, *solutions proposed on one side or another may be easily confused by many people with the gospel message* (43).

In order that laymen among the faithful should know this, it is necessary that the clergy among the faithful know it. In this the Vatican Council did not fail. Therefore it did not fail in its primary task of articulating afresh the ethical and social implications of the Christian message in today's world. It was not led away from this by an unholy zeal to enforce some particular solution or, for that matter, by a legitimate sense of the urgency that solutions be obtained if at all possible.

Since the point to be stressed here is the methodology of ecumenical messages, it is not necessary here to examine how well the "Pastoral Constitution on the Church in the Modern World" succeeded in speaking to the world today without ceasing to be the church speaking, or how well it succeeded in splitting the difference between somewhat general statements and particular recommendations and yet spoke *relevantly* a much needed word to all mankind. I have elsewhere analyzed the magnitude of the accomplishment of the council in addressing itself to the problem of modern warfare.[7] This helpfully informs and forms the consciences of men on the basis of Christian and moral insights, without committing them or the church to particular solutions concerning which there may be legitimate debate.

Perhaps it should be mentioned that there is an easily overlooked additional virtue in striving always to speak for the whole church and for the entirety of Christian insights in whatever is addressed to the church and to the world about today's problems. This is that none of the sons of the church should be forgotten in our zeal for particular solutions. The "Message to the Churches" adopted by the General Board of the NCC, accompanying its Policy Statement on Vietnam, stated the conviction: "We believe that war in this nuclear age settles hardly anything and may destroy everything." By omitting to say more, one could infer from this that those sons of the church are the more to be pitied who serve in the armed forces; that, while belonging to the church by conversion to Christ and baptism in his name, theirs is a most dubious vocation, or hardly at all a Christian vocation.

The Vatican Council said the same thing and with equal force about modern warfare, but without failing to speak *to* and *for* these sons of the church also. It urged that men need to "strain every muscle" (82) to outlaw war and uproot it by establishing new public institutions on a world scale. It rightly called the present deterrent peace of the world "unsteady," indeed only "peace of a sort." It correctly estimated the horror and immorality of war today if it should be total. But it did not forget to say that "those who are pledged to the service of their country as members of its armed forces should regard themselves as agents of security and freedom on behalf of their people. As long as they fulfill this role properly, they are making a genuine contribution to the establishment of peace" (79). Thus did all these sons of the church find a place in the church speaking. The church spoke for them as well as to them or about them because it endeavored to speak the full Christian social doctrine more than it proposed to save the political leaders of the nations from having to make their own prudential political decisions.

Protestant pronouncements not only often fail to remember the sons of the church serving in the armed forces. In their eagerness to strike out in the direction of correcting the structural defects of the nation-state system, they sometimes make judgments upon war that entail the verdict that anyone in the armed services is doing something that is either *unjust* or *irrelevant,* or both. Only they do not take responsibility, by this verdict, for frankly recommending that the church become a "sect" in regard to all military establishments, and for urging that Christians selectively withdraw from the political and altogether from the military sectors of our societies. Thus, the Policy Statement of the Council for Christian Social Action of the United Church of Christ, February, 1965, pronounced, without any qualification for the "meanwhile," the "irrelevance" of war; and in a few paragraphs it established the injustice of any political use of force except in UN police actions. "In the contemporary situation," it declared, "war can meet neither of these requirements" [proportionate means and a reasonable chance of success]; and it concluded that any war under any circumstances in today's world "is stripped of such moral sanction as Christians have accorded the just war." [8] By contrast, the Vatican Council was able to place equal moral force behind the need for new directions in international politics and the need for world public authority, without being betrayed into making demonstrably

133

false statements about Christian responsibility in the meanwhile before these are established, and without being forced to an evident abandonment to dereliction, irrelevance, or injustice those sons of the church whose vocations are in the military.

This continued to be the case at Geneva. The only paragraph in the entire report directed to sons of the church who serve in "civil and military organization" was, even before revision, an exceedingly grudging and meager one. This said, after a paragraph addressed to those who withdraw or act upon the established order from without: "However, a majority of Christians believe themselves called to work within the existing order for its transformation and accept a role in its civil and military organization." That at least allowed for the positive importance of serving the state's preserving function and defending the justice embodied in the nation. This was, not insignificantly, changed to read: "A majority of Christians, in working within the existing order, believe themselves called to work for its transformation and accept a role in its civil and military organization." The productive and transforming work of Christians within the existing order is a not unimportant reason for their being there; but surely their vocation in the state's conserving function, and in defense, ought not to be slighted. The statement concluded: "They must never lose sight of its [the existing order's] inherent imperfection which is obscured by the self-deceptions that come from within it, for then they will maintain a constant pressure for progress." [9] Surely a way could be found in speaking for and to all the sons of the church simply to affirm that service in the armed forces is a calling in which Christians should regard themselves as agents of justice and freedom; and without seeming to imply that self-deception comes from the fact that one is working within the existing order any more than this may come from the fact that in the service of justice and freedom one has chosen to oppose it.

It is strikingly evident that as we become increasingly oriented upon one particular thing we want to speak to the churches ("prevent war"), we articulate less and less the full Christian understanding of politics and at the same time have less and less to say to all the sons of the churches everywhere, e.g., the vocation of Christians in the armed forces in the service of justice and freedom. This is a significant defect in the Geneva report, especially when placed beside the fact that the conference was fulsome and rather unqualified in its praise of nonviolent direct action and approved in more than oblique fashion of the political use of violence in revolutionary causes.[10] Indeed, not having statable moral limits other than the justice of the cause to be placed upon revolutionary violence is a result of having first driven too deeply into one's soul the quite mistaken notion that nonviolent direct action is somehow bound to be inherently moral or Christian if only the cause is just. By contrast, the Vatican Council was able to surround both nonviolence and service in the armed forces with the same requirements, if still somewhat minimal requirements: "Motivated by this same spirit ["to practice the truth in love" (Eph. 4:15)], we cannot fail to praise those who renounce the use of violence in the vindication of their rights and who resort to methods of defense which are otherwise available to weaker parties too, *provided that this can be done without injury to the rights and duties of others or of the community itself*" (78).

It is time for stock-taking. It is high time for it to be acknowledged on all sides that not every decision is a moral decision, and not every moral decision is a Christian decision. The bearing of God's will and governance in relation to every aspect of human life cannot possibly be construed in such fashion that supposes that there is a Christian shape or style to every decision. Concerning a great many choices it has to be said that only a deliberately or inflexibly imprudent decision would be wrong, or an uncharitable exercise of prudence. The principle of prudence (among a Christian's teachings) definitely refers the matter in question to the magistrate or to the political process for decision; and Christians as such can say no more than that this is the case.

The hour is coming, and now is, for all of us to recognize the truth of something Rabbi Arthur Hertsberg of Kansas City wrote in the *National Catholic Reporter* (December 17, 1965).

It is easy enough to defend priests and rabbis, and sometimes even columnists and editors, in their right to hold opinions, rooted in their spiritual convictions, about the problems of the day. There is in such a defense a rekindling of our high dedication to freedom. Nonetheless, it is particularly important for political and theological liberals to remember that there is at least one other dimension to the situation. The relevance of religion in the modern world cannot mean that there is a direct and clear mandate from God either to get into South Vietnam further or to get out entirely or to recognize Red China tomorrow morning.

And recognizing this to be the case, it is time for us to begin to act accordingly in the pronouncements of religious bodies and groups of Christians upon public questions. Especially in this ecumenical age, it is necessary to know that even a universal religious community would not be a world political community with the competence to determine such matters or any special competence to recommend these specific decisions (or to recommend the opposite policies,

136

which by the *same* error "conservative" Christians hold to be within their religio-political province).

It is often said in defense of specific recommendations or condemnations that churchmen can agree on these without being in agreement on the theological, the ethical, or even the political *reasons* for them; and that the important thing is the agreement on policy. This is true in a political community, where persons with different theological points of view, different denominations, and different political and other philosophies have covenanted to live together by the agreements they can come to out of the political processes in force, and to live with the results of the execution of such agreements. Precisely this is not the case in the world church; this forms no continuing community of political policy formation and execution in which we live by agreements that submerge many fundamental differences and live with the results of the execution of such agreements. Instead, we all went home from Geneva to *live the state*[11] among many different peoples. Here our different reasons for saying particular things that shape our political community and its action sometimes do not much matter. There in Geneva our different reasons for saying particular things, especially the marks upon us of the nations from which we came, mattered very much in faulting, or not, the particular agreements. What if faulty theology or an inadequate understanding of Christian social ethics helped to sustain one or another of these specifics? Gathered together not to ask the fundamental questions concerning the social ethics that should be the church speaking, we at the same time could not have been placed upon our mettle in reaching specific agreements ("whatever else Christians might believe") by the fact that we knew we were a continuing political community living such agreements into execution.

In order for the church to regain *its* voice and for the churches or Christians in council to speak for the church to the world today, we must resist the temptation to believe that what needs to be done is to improve the church's use of "experts." It is the aim of specificity in the church's resolutions and proclamations that should be radically called in question. The better use of political and other experts to improve *that* might only make matters worse. On the other hand, it is certainly true that the church's *deliberations* and our procedures for deliberation need to be reexamined.

The notion that laymen who are experts, for example, in the political and economic sciences can enable the church to speak a relevant Christian word to today's world and at the same time to point out the particular policy to be followed is simply an illusion. It takes an expert to pick an expert. Or rather the experts disagree; and if there is any reason at all and not just an accident why one set of experts and not another comes to council, the decision concerning which ones are to be picked to inform church councils will inevitably be made by some *curia* or persons in control of setting up such councils in terms of the particular interests, positions, or trends of thought the experts are already reputed for. This is not exactly the way basically to improve deliberation (although it may be one way to determine which specifics should be specifically uttered). Unless and until we clarify our minds about what we mean to be doing about the church's proper address to questions of social ethics, no amount or kind of radical improvement in the church's deliberations and its conference procedures will tell us how to be the church speaking on any particular question, no matter how many experts there are. Selection from among available political analysts will be an arbitrary one so long as particularity is in view. And when the church's goals in social ethics, its deliberations, and its procedures for deliberation are corrected, the movement will not be any longer in the direction of presuming to give specific prudential advice to political leaders, but rather in the direction of regaining the church's own voice relevant to today's problems.

The most penetrating discussion to date of the problem we are dealing with is Ralph Potter's "Silence or Babel: the Churches and Peace." [12] Yet in the end he yields to the lure of expertise rather than give up the social gospel–contextual notion that the church as such should be speaking specific words on the specific issues of public policy. He only penetrates the problem deeply enough to see that there would have to be an entire "new breed" of experts in the service of the church[13]—each, or each group of them, giving himself (if I do not read Potter incorrectly) in scandalous particularity to the mastery of a given social problem (other churchmen taking his word for it). He is propelled to this conclusion because he seems to believe that the only alternatives are his own proposal, the present level of competence in the church's specific pronouncements, or resting "content to speak only at the highest level of generality." [14] These I have sought to deny are the choices; and to say that in between is the authentic area of the articulation of Christian social ethics which is the church's single task in speaking to the world today. Can it really be believed that a popery of the expert, whose particular voice shortly becomes the church's recommendation, no matter how expert he is, would be the way to improve the present popery of committees and conferences? This might add some merit to the church's policy-making exercises, but it would be no improvement in the church speaking.

It is necessary to turn in quite another direction, to improve the church's deliberations *as church,* to advance the deliberations of Christians as Christians, to establish

139

some universe of discourse among Christian ethicists and at church conferences. (The field of Christian social ethics, as this is done by professionals today, is in as much disarray as social ethics in the ecumenical churches.) It is *deliberation* upon the social and ethical implications of the Christian faith that is most lacking today, not particular recommendations (which can be drawn forthwith from the faith by at least everyone and thereupon urged upon all). Not even church-sponsored social action is the issue, but before that the *proper* deliberation!

The Vatican Council tried, at least, to express the entirety of the Christian understanding relevant to any particular problem that needs to be articulated freshly and soundly and impressed anew upon the mind of the church and in the public mind; it did not attempt the particular solution of problems, however urgent. If this is not the direction we take, the result will be that there will be more and more specific recommendations and less and less of Christian substance informing our ecumenical councils and remaining in our culture. It is a yen for specific involvement that betrays us from our primary calling, and from the world's most urgent need. This can be said, without denying that the distinction is only a relative one between "specific" statements and "general" statements if the latter are truly relevant to the problem in question.

Of course, we need also to face directly the problem of integrating the work of theological, political, and other experts with the resolutions and pronouncements issued by church councils if there is to be a real improvement in the deliberative procedures by which we propose to speak as Christians and as Christian churches or boards to the world today. My modest procedural proposal would be that, for a moment at least, Vatican Council II be taken seriously as a model. In meetings on Church and Society sponsored in the past by the NCC and the WCC there has always been a solid body of work done by theological and other experts in the production of "preparatory volumes." Then came the council, meeting in a single session, which made certain findings and resolutions. This was the pattern again for the Geneva Conference in 1966. Four preparatory volumes were published,[15] and there was some reference made at the conference to a few of the chapters in these volumes. But the work of the *periti,* the experts, is not well enough integrated, or hardly integrated at all, into the deliberations of the councils of churchmen sponsored by the older ecumenical movement—not nearly so well as was the case at Vatican II.

To do this will require that several sessions be held of the same council over a period of years. There must be time for the "fathers of the church" in council to study the work prepared beforehand by experts; and during the sessions, ways must be found for the official participants to hear and question the experts, to discuss with them the meaning of draft statements in process of being prepared for adoption. There needs to be some way to indicate to committees and experts alike the trend or inchoate mind of the council, and time between sessions for substantive theological-ethical work to be done on the drafting. Several sessions are needed for there to be ample debate on the floor, and for revision and re-revision of any statement that is finally promulgated.

Still these or suchlike procedural reforms will be of no avail unless and until we in the older ecumenical movement regain the understanding that it is the Christian life and Christian action we are trying to clarify, and help one another clarify, in today's world. It is the genius of Protestantism to elevate in importance the layman, while it is the genius of Catholicism to emphasize expert knowledge. The Second Vatican Council was, in fact, a great council because the theologians exerted an influence as never before upon shaping the mind of the Bishops in council; the *periti* were "experts" in *Christian understanding,* and not just experts. There is, in contrast, an intractable difficulty in the way of advancing Protestant ecumenical ethics because of our exaltation of the lay expert, in an age when lay Christians have so largely ceased to exercise the universal ministry of the faithful, the priesthood of all believers to one another, in witnessing to one another concerning the meaning of Christ for our lives. This is another reason why procedural improvements, and the involvement of laymen who have expert knowledge of the world's problems, are not likely to do much good. Unless the goals of our meeting together, on the part of clergy and laymen alike, can somehow be changed, we are not likely to grow in the strength to be the church speaking —Christians as such speaking to one another the living Word and only those words that can be spoken on this basis to one another and to the world today. At stake in bringing to an end the era of theological-ethical "prefaces" to precise secular pronouncements is the restoration of Christian substance in all our understandings.[16] The one cannot be done without the other also.

There is also a model at hand in the older ecumenical movement itself. Let "Church and Society" look to what "Faith and Order" has been doing lately. In the years prior to the first meeting and actual organization of the WCC at Amsterdam in 1948, and preparatory to this, both these "departments" in the life of the churches had done basic and original research and thinking together in the area of our understanding of the faith of the church, its polity, ministry, and sacraments, and its social ethics. Quite understandably, in the years pointing immediately to the First Assembly of the WCC and especially in the years following the achievement of this much unity of thought and action among the churches, we were content and had to be content with treading water at a more superficial level, simply agreeing as to our disagreements without much continuing effort to push into and beyond them lest the fragile bases for unity be too much disturbed. "Faith and Order" concentrated on questions of order, of ministry and sacraments, and thus could only expose the existing disagreements. It was felt that to go behind these to fundamental questions of faith would be too disturbing and might lead to the exposure of irresolvable differences among the churches and to even greater felt disunity.

"The Responsible Society" was itself a compromise concept that deliberately set to one side the different theological-ethical warrants for this summary agreement on the meaning of social responsibility, which then could be used in specific recommendations or incriminations. The vogue to date of seeking agreement on particulars, whatever be our reasons, and however divergent these may be, lives off a reluctance to reopen fundamental issues in ecumenical ethics. In this Geneva 1966 introduced no change: procedurally the conference could not do so, and intentionally it looked in the direction away from the theological and ethical foundations of ecumenism in the vain hope of finding elsewhere the church's message to the world today.

Meantime, something of a renewal has taken place in Faith and Order discussions in the last fifteen years—since the Third World Conference on Faith and Order at Lund in 1952. Fundamental questions have been taken up again, no one knowing what the results will be, or the shape that may be given to the thinking and the life of the churches in the future if various understandings of the faith of the

143

church are placed again in the center of attention. Lund initiated an effort "to set out from the center which had been given to us all, to study Christology together, and then to understand anew the differences which separate us in the foreground." Some sort of Christology, as we have seen, was the inchoate theology at Geneva 1966, but this was an *arrière-pensée,* not placed in the center of attention. In its renewed address to the fundamentals of faith, "Faith and Order" discovered in the post-Lund period that Christology was not the only center given us from which to understand anew such matters as ministry and sacrament, but that the entirety of classical Christian theology is involved as well.

In all this the leaders of "Faith and Order" were going consciously against the stream, and against the apprehensions of many churchmen, in order to find a way through the simple agreement about our solid disagreements at the level of church order. In "Church and Society" the problem is superficial agreements in social and political ethics, for all sorts of unexamined reasons. Here too one must be willing to go against the stream, to probe again the fundamental issues of faith and life. If, in Christian social ethics, dogmatics is ethics and ethics is dogmatics, there is as much need for "Church and Society" to begin with the bases given us in ethics and then to understand anew the light that can be thrown upon the urgent problems in the foreground, as there was for "Faith and Order" to begin again with the faith before renewing an attack on particular problems of church unity. Why cannot the following be said *mutatis mutandis* of "Church and Society" as surely as this was a decisive turning point for "Faith and Order"?

In our search for greater unity we must turn to the questions which determine the whole of theology. We must clarify first the deepest questions, we must examine the presuppositions upon which the whole of life and doctrine of the church is built; and only then can we apply ourselves to the specific questions, which we have not yet been able to set aside. If we deal first with the specific problems, we end up inevitably in culs-de-sac. For the specific problems refuse to be treated apart from the deeper questions. The fruitless discussions about the ministry and intercommunion bear all too clear witness to this.[17]

In accomplishing its own renewal, "Faith and Order" adopted procedures for common study more apt to produce profound common thinking concerning questions of faith. These too might provide "Church and Society" with something of a model if ever the decision is made to forgo policy-making exercises and to seek instead to advance and deepen our understanding of ecumenical social ethics and to promote this in the life of the churches and, so far as may be, in the world of today. There were organized a great many study groups meeting over a period of two years, seeking to identify ingredients of the problem in the church's understanding of its faith and to promote the needed research, before the North American Conference on Faith and Order was held at Oberlin in 1957. The same procedure was adopted on other continents; and after Oberlin this worldwide study among representatives of various denominations continued up to the meeting of the Fourth World Conference on Faith and Order at Montreal in 1964.

It cannot be imagined that by any less effort, and without trying together to find out what we mean when we Christians engage in ecumenical ethical speaking, we can have anything to say to the churches or to the world of today. The analogy with "Faith and Order" insistently came to mind in Geneva in the midst of the all too weighty

145

responsibility placed on this conference and in face of what was expected and hoped would be its issue.

Some such procedures as these are needed before ever the churches, or their ecumenical meetings, can reasonably be expected to be in some sense the church speaking. How else can churchmen speak upon the foundation of the whole of Christian truth and insights in a relevant way to the churches and to the world today? I do not know what would emerge from the improvement of the process of Christian deliberation. Doubtless the substance of the ethics would be different from the substance of the Roman Catholic ethics we have examined. Still, if the procedures can be devised that can match the deliberative procedures of the Vatican Council (or for that matter the concern for the fullness of Christian truth that is attained by the processes by which a social encyclical is issued by a pontiff), or if we can find a way of discussing the church and political or social questions with the same depth and substance that have been given to recent church deliberations about Faith and Order, perhaps then one could be sure it is *Christian* social ethics that will be done.[18]

Moreover, a conscious effort must be made to overcome the "structural defect" by which "Faith and Order" is separated from "Church and Society." It cannot be argued that ecumenical ethics has any other foundation than the Christian faith, or that the ethics we should be doing and speaking to the churches and to the world is any the less, or less directly, founded in elements of the Christian faith than church order, sacraments, and the ministry. Yet these two departments are set apart. This encourages the view that Christian teachings to the world of today can be formulated properly without tracing them home to Christian warrants and without limiting "Church and Society" pronouncements to whatever can be said with such warrants.

146

If not by taking thought, if not by some self-denying ordinance placed upon the churches' speaking, then an effort must be made to correct this structural defect which makes for a separation between our social teachings and the faith of the church. This can be accomplished as easily as the responsible leaders of secular society can lend an ear to us and begin to correct the structural defects of the nation-state system! Until both are accomplished, the leaders of church and state alike must be doing something wrong, despite all the goodwill they may possess—or at least they must not be doing something right.

This does not mean that a church council can be infallible or indefectible. As a Protestant, I, at least, am resolved to stand with Luther against both pope and council, or the pope in council, Visser 't Hooft in council, or Blake in council, unless I can be shown from Scripture and sound reason. No amount or kind of procedural improvement will suffice if some of the goals of "Church and Society" remain. Still, unless far sounder deliberation can be secured by a greater "institutionalized" interplay between Christian theology and an ecumenical ethics for today's world, a serious student of these matters cannot but regard the resolutions of churchmen on any number of urgent specific questions with increasing dismay—or as a laughing matter. That is, if the love of Christ and his church permits the exercise of a sense of humor when what is at stake is witness to this light in the present world, and not the prudential solutions of other problems, however urgent.

THE CHURCH
AND THE MAGISTRATE[1]

Former Secretary of State Dean Acheson made a remarkable and markedly misunderstood address on "Ethics in
International Relations Today" at Amherst College on
December 9, 1964. "In foreign affairs," he said, "only
the end can justify the means." He immediately went on
to say: "This is not to say that the end justifies any means,
or that some ends can justify anything."

Mr. Acheson naturally placed first the guiding rule that
must be uppermost in a statesman's mind. In furniture
making a chair is made to be sat in. So in policy making, a
particular policy is made to be lived by. One must be able to
live with or live better with the totality of its results.

In international affairs, the means available are always
tragically limited by the fact that not all that ought to be
can be politically done, or can be done by us. Any alternative leaves undone some good or does some evil to match
the good achieved; and it can always be contended after the
fact that one or another of the alternatives refused might
have been better.

In this, making foreign policy is somewhat different
from making a chair. Since this is the case, only the end or
the carefully calculated main effect can justify all the other
effects let loose in the world, or never brought to realization, when a statesman lights upon some particular policy
or chooses his means. In this sense *only* the end can ever
justify the putting forth of available political means. It is
the business of political magistrates to see to this as they
rule by particular decrees.

But Mr. Acheson went on to say that, of course, the

end does not justify *any* means, nor can some ends justify anything. It would be possible to set before government the adoption of goals that are such that they would justify nothing in the realm of means, and it is possible for some means to be proposed that could be justified by nothing in the realm of ends. Presumably, also, the statesman has in his head or knows in his conscience something about the means that no end—and about the ends that no means —can warrant. Among the legitimate means and ends of politics, therefore, only the end can justify the means.

Our society needs continual reflection upon political doctrine and the nature of politics; it needs an understanding and articulation of its proper means and ends. This alone can form and strengthen the context in which the policy maker puts into practice the truth that only ends can justify the decisions and actions he puts forth.

If the churches have any special wisdom to offer here, it is in cultivating the political ethos of a nation and informing the conscience of the statesman. The church's business is not policy formation. That is the awesome responsibility of magistrates (and of churchmen along with other citizens in their nonecclesiastical capacities).

I am aware that the foregoing may sound different from the way Mr. Acheson was heard. His address was an attack upon the discussion of ethics in connection with politics, which he termed "a prolific cause of confusion"; and he asserted that "what passes for ethical standards for government policies in foreign policies is a collection of moralisms, maxims, and slogans which neither help nor guide but only confuse decision."

In one passage he elevated the national interest to supremacy in a fashion permitting a narrow conception that no churchman and no proper view of politics can accept. In connection with too many specific policy decisions chosen for illustration, he said that "moral talk did not bear on the problem"—though that is true enough of the "moral talk" heard today. And he seemed to assert that because "nations are not individuals," this means that they are "governed by wholly different considerations."

Yet when the former Secretary reflected that "the same conduct is not moral under all circumstances," he clearly said that "its *moral* propriety seems to depend . . . upon the relationship of those concerned with the conduct" (italics added). This is like saying that the morality of marriage depends upon the nature of the relationship, and not upon some abstract maxims from which one seeks to deduce proper conduct in marriage; or like asking whether individuals are fit for marriage instead of saying that marriage may be good for individuals; it is like asking whether individual conduct is right in terms of "the relationship of those concerned with the conduct."

Similarly, to ask whether politics is good for an aggregation of individuals or to make political judgments as if for persons apart from the nature of politics would be a moralism insufficiently attentive to the relationship that actually exists between the individuals and the nations concerned with the conduct. Such moralism Mr. Acheson rightly rejected.

But he did not exclude a proper ethics from a place in politics. In fact he asserted that "to further enduring good relations between states," international relations themselves require that political conduct be "designed to inspire trust and confidence." "To achieve this result," he is convinced, "the conduct of diplomacy should conform to the same moral and ethical principles which inspire trust and confidence when followed by and between individuals." Moreover, he was no more opposed to the "deduction" of foreign policy from "ethical and moral principles" than he is to "modern

150

Machiavellis" who would conduct politics without any regard to moral principles.

It seems to me that this address makes a great amount of sense if we keep clear the fact that Mr. Acheson is opposing the propensity of religious people and most other Americans to mark down the notations "moral" or "immoral" beside the specific policy decisions of magistrates without first considering the nature of politics. This does not mean that morality should be left to the experts in ethics or that the ordinary man is not competent to make moral judgments. But it does mean that the leaders of opinion, whether ethicists or not, who presume to articulate and influence the moral opinion of a nation and to use "moral talk" in the public forum are responsible for some disciplined reflection.

It is an appalling fact that the more the substance of the moral life disappears from our culture and the more hosts of people are alienated from politics, the more these words are bandied around. I am afraid that Mr. Acheson has simply heard too much loose talk about what's moral and what's immoral brought to bear upon particular political policies by critics who substitute such language for careful analysis.

Even Mr. Acheson himself was too much bound by such usage at one point and found himself too hesitant to break with fashion. He could hardly bring himself to call "immoral" something he very clearly believes to be a political immorality. After asking the question, "Is it moral to deny ourselves the use of force in all circumstances?" he replied that this would be a "bad bargain" and a "stupid" one. He then added, with a seeming great reluctance to state the plain truth, "I would almost say an immoral one."

This is at least the moral truth that is clear to Mr. Acheson; his hesitancy to say so shows only the degree to which he has taken his understanding of the morality of

151

politics from the moralism he opposes. He immediately went on to state his deep conviction that "the very conception of morality seems to involve a duty to preserve values outside the contour of our own skins, and at the expense of forgoing much that is desired and pleasant, including—it may be—our own fortunes and lives."

If churchmen want to put an end to the moralism that only confuses political decision, we will need to do more than oppose the personal ethics of Protestant individualism when made into standards for official conduct. We will also have to put an end to the political ethics of the "liberal consensus"—built up by a great number of position papers and resolutions on *specific policy decisions*—that attach the labels "right" or "wrong," "moral" or "immoral," to innumerable particular choices of the statesman about which churchmen *as such* know less than he.

It is not the church's business to recommend but only to clarify the grounds upon which the statesman must put forth his own particular decree. Christian political ethics cannot say what should or must be done but only what may be done. It can only try to make sure that false doctrine does not unnecessarily trammel policy choices or preclude decisions that might better shape and govern events.

In politics the church is only a *theoretician*. The religious communities as such should be concerned with *perspectives* upon politics, with political doctrine, with the direction and structures of the common life, not with specific directives. They should seek to clarify and keep wide open the legitimate options for choice, and thus nurture the moral and political ethos of the nation. Their task is not the determination of policy. Their special orientation upon politics is, in a sense, an exceedingly limited one; yet an exceedingly important one. Still, in this they need to stand in awe before people called political "decision makers," or rather before the majesty of topmost political agency.

Political decision and action is an image of the majesty of God, who also rules by particular decrees. God says, "Let there be . . ."; and his word becomes deed and actuality. So also earthly magistrates have the high and lonely responsibility of declaring what shall actually be done. Allowing for the limitations that surround even the highest magistrate of a great nation, it is still the case that he creatively shapes events by decisions that must be particular decisions going beyond doctrine. He must actualize what is to be from among a number of legitimate choices.

The majesty of political rulership is that it is always a triumph over doctrine through right doctrine, a victory over generalities through the proper generalities and through the proper direction of policy. Political rulership makes life-giving, or at least actuality-giving, deeds out of words. This does not mean that the magistrates, or Christians acting as citizens, are always wise. It means only that they are magistrates, which the church is not.

The religious communities have a less awe-full responsibility; their task is a less- or a non-magisterial one: it is to see to it that the word over which and through which statesmanship or government wins its victory is not an inadequate word. When the churches turn their primary attention to trying to influence particular policy decisions, they do what they ought not to do.

Churches today are becoming very legalistic about what they regard as a consensus of moral and religious opinion built up by the precedents established through a series of position papers on *particular* policy questions. I think it cannot be denied that these resolutions have exceedingly questionable foundation in either theological ethics or political doctrine. This is Protestant *casuistry,* and its fault is

153

not to be excused by virtue of its exclusion of conservative personal ethics from importation into politics.

In adopting a casuistry of building up Christian social teachings out of the precedents of past particular decisions, the churches are in danger of leaving undone what they ought to do. They should clarify the ground on which government must rest. They ought to open wide the articulation of structural elements in that human reality which statesmanship must govern and the range of alternatives it is legitimate for statesmen to have in mind as they rule by specific decree. They should inform the ethos and conscience of the nation, and thus aid in forming the conscience of its statesmen.

Moreover, by doing what they ought not to do and leaving undone what they ought to have done, the churches may well contribute to the formation of particular decisions that ought never to be done. This sometimes happens when previous ecclesiastical pronouncements, themselves too specific, are legalistically cited. Christian political ethics has a contribution to make precisely by keeping open the range of multifactoral principles or objectives that impinge upon a statesman's choices. Surely Protestant Christians, whose consciences are not bound by either pope or church councils, ought to be engaged constantly in going to the theoretical roots in the examination and reexamination of any and all ecclesiastical pronouncements, instead of using these as legal instruments for keeping in repair some supposed consensus on particular policies.

I have stressed the implicit wisdom and moral direction the churches might contribute to a statesman's enormously difficult decisions if they paid attention to that which they may know something about instead of adding to the confusion of particular decisions, or weakening his hand or strengthening it in the wrong direction, by pronouncing

154

directly upon the choices before a magistrate as he rules by particular decrees. This is, finally a rectification of no little importance for the church's own inner life.

Professor John C. Bennett received a number of letters from obviously sincere and not unintelligent or immoral people who felt they had been practically unchurched by the way a consensus of church pronouncements had been used on them in the 1964 presidential campaign. Writing in *Christianity and Crisis* (December 28, 1964) after the election, Dr. Bennett "emphasized that a distinction must be made between the basic Christian convictions that bind a member to his church and the opinions of church bodies on particular issues." Can anyone doubt that this distinction was made too little *during* the campaign by liberals and conservatives alike? [2]

Can anyone doubt that we have a long way to go before the church gives itself the machinery (or gets rid of some) by which it can become a community of unlimited discussion and discourse about what Scripture and sound reason require of us in the general direction of political affairs in the present day? A community in which the "littlest he" or the most conservative one has his Christian life to lead as well as the rest of us. A community in which someone —anyone—may have something significant to say to us contrary to anything that has yet been said, correcting or increasing the light we think we now have or directing it upon some as yet unexposed part of the path men and nations must now tread.

At the moment this nation still has before it agonizing decisions in regard to South Vietnam. Not only the topmost magistrate but every citizen (including every churchman) has to make up his mind on this urgent question. But what can the church *as church* know about this? Moreover, whatever is wise or foolish in our specific military actions

155

or political and negotiating posture in this particular instance is not going to help us decide similar questions the next time we confront insurgency warfare or in deciding where and how to make our presence felt in Asia. There is no point in trying to compile a Christian social ethic by leapfrogging from one problem to another.

The political conscience of the nation would be aided more, and particular decisions more instructed, if there were fewer judgments emanating from the churches upon specific cases, delivered as if these were the only conclusions to be reached from considerations of morality. The nation and the statesman would be more edified by currents of discussion about the immorality and probable ineffectiveness of nonintervention to balance the talk about the immorality and probable ineffectiveness of intervention. There should be discussion of the responsibilities of a nation because the United Nations is such a weak reed, as well as talk of our duty to strengthen world organizations. Moreover, no one should talk about the difficulties and failures confronting purposeful intervention without also talking about the difficulties and failures of "coalition" governments (Laos).

Christians should be speaking more about order as a terminal political value along with justice, without the naïve assumption that these are bound to go together without weight given to both. More about the need for the rule of law as well as revolutionary change. Of serving human liberty as well as the war on poverty, without the presumption that there is an "invisible hand" that links these together in the absence of specific attention to each. About the individual and community values at stake in destroying the illusion that government will provide a solution for every irritant or distress, as well as what government can and should do. Of the responsible use of political power as

156

well as the limits upon it. Of how involvement in the world's problems means tragic involvement.

And there needs to be among Christians a consensus that in the concrete life of charity we should never aspire or even imagine that we are going to get rid of our neighbor's need in such wise as to get rid of our enduringly needy neighbors.

As a citizen one may lean to one extreme or the other in this range of options. As churchmen, however, our concern should be that the range of relevant principles be not narrowed, and that the conscience of the nation and of the statesman be not deprived of perspectives and wisdom that may be needed elements in the decisions magistrates have to make.

Let the church be the church and let the magistrate be the magistrate. Let both keep their distances. May there be less confusion of these roles. Let the President advance policies without playing priest-king to the people in exercising his ruling under God's overruling. Let the churches advise the magistrates under their care in less specific terms, while always renewing in them the perspectives—*all* the perspectives—upon the political order that Christianity affords. And let us pray more for those in authority (not the churches as such) who must shape the future by what they decree, and who in doing so must step creatively into an uncertain future beyond the range of any light that has been or can ever be thrown upon their pathway.

APPENDIX A
THE OXFORD CONFERENCE[1]
1937

THE CHURCH AND WAR

We approach this part of our subject with a profound sense of its urgency and of the inadequacy of the best that we can say. We know that multitudes are oppressed by the actual menace of war. While we may seek to influence actions which may avert the immediate danger, our main task is to probe the underlying sources of the evil and point to the ultimate remedy.

Here again our starting point is the universal fellowship of Christians, the *una sancta*. All Christians acknowledge one Lord, whose claim upon them is such as to transcend all other loyalties. Here is the first obligation of the church, to be in living fact the church, a society with a unity so deep as to be indestructible by earthly divisions of race or nation or class.

Wars, the occasions of war, and all situations which conceal the fact of conflict under the guise of outward peace, are marks of a world to which the church is charged to proclaim the gospel of redemption. War involves compulsory enmity, diabolical outrage against human personality, and a wanton distortion of the truth. War is a particular demonstration of the power of sin in this world and a defiance of the righteousness of God as revealed in Jesus Christ and him crucified. No justification of war must be allowed to conceal or minimize this fact.

158

In all situations the Christian has to bear in mind both the absolute command, "Thou shalt love thy neighbor as thyself," and the obligation to do what most nearly corresponds to that command in the circumstances confronting him. His action may be but a poor expression of perfect love; the man is caught in a sinful situation, to the evil of which he may have contributed much or little. The best that is possible falls far "short of the glory of God" and is, in that sense, sinful; each man must bear his share of the corporate sin which has rendered impossible any better course; and we all have to confess that "our righteousnesses are as filthy rags." Yet to do what appears as relatively best is an absolute duty before God, and to fail in this is to incur positive guilt.

The search for the will of God is a matter of agonizing perplexity for the Christian whose country is involved in war. We have to recognize two widely divergent views regarding war, along with several that are intermediate. One view hopes for the elimination of war by the power of God working in history through the religious and moral enlightenment of men and the exercise of their free wills; the other view regards man as so bound in the necessities of a sinful world that war will be eliminated only as a consequence of the return of Christ in glory.

In practice this divergence issues in three main positions which are sincerely and conscientiously held by Christians:

(1) Some believe that war, especially in its modern form, is always sin, being a denial of the nature of God as love, of the redemptive way of the cross, and of the community of the Holy Spirit; that war is always ultimately destructive in its effects, and ends in futility by corrupting even the noblest purpose for which it is waged; and that the church will become a creative, regenerative and reconciling instrument for the healing of the nations only as it renounces war absolutely. They are therefore constrained to refuse to take part in war themselves, to plead among their fellows for a similar repudiation of war in favor of a better way, and to replace military force by methods of active peacemaking.

159

(2) Some would participate only in "just wars." Here there are at least two points of view, depending upon the definition of the "just war." The first view holds that Christians should participate only in such wars as are justifiable on the basis of international law. They believe that in a sinful world the state has the duty, under God, to use force when law and order are threatened. Wars against transgressors of international agreements and pacts are comparable with police measures and Christians are obliged to participate in them. But if the state requires its citizens to participate in wars which cannot be thus justified, they believe that Christians should refuse, for the state has no right to force its citizens to take part in sinful actions. Many would add that no war should be regarded as "just" if the government concerned fails to submit the subject of dispute or *casus belli* to arbitration, conciliation or judgment of an international authority.

Those who hold the second view would regard a "just war" as one waged to vindicate what they believe to be an essential Christian principle: to defend the victims of wanton aggression or to secure freedom for the oppressed. They would urge that it was a Christian duty, where all other means had failed, to take up arms. In so doing they would look to the verdict of conscience as their ultimate sanction. While recognizing the general importance of supporting civil or international order, the maintenance of such order in the present imperfect state of society cannot be a final obligation. The Christian, though he must be willing to accept martyrdom for himself, cannot expose others to it by refusing to fight for them.

(3) Some, while also stressing the Christian obligation to work for peace and mutual understanding among the nations, hold nevertheless that no such effort can end war in this world. Moreover, while recognizing that political authority is frequently administered in a selfish and immoral way, they nevertheless believe that the state is the agent divinely appointed to preserve a nation from the detrimental effects of anarchic and criminal tendencies among its members, and to maintain its existence against the aggression of its neighbors.

It is therefore a Christian's duty to obey the political authority as far as possible and to refrain from everything that is apt to weaken it. This means that normally a Christian must take up arms for his country. Only when he is absolutely certain that his country is fighting for a wrong cause—for example, in case of unjustifiable war of aggression—has the ordinary citizen a right to refuse military service.

Of those who hold this view, some would admit that individuals may be called directly by God to refuse categorically to take part in any war and so draw attention to the perverted nature of a world in which wars are possible. In either case the individual must recognize in principle the significance of the state and be willing to accept punishment by the authorities for violating the national law.

We do not affirm that any one of these positions can be held to represent the only possible Christian attitude. The church must insist that the perplexity itself is a sign of the sin in which its members are implicated. It cannot rest in permanent acquiescence in the continuance of these differences but should do all that is possible to promote the study of the problem by people of different views meeting together to learn from one another as they seek to understand the purpose of God as revealed in Jesus Christ. Recognizing that its members are also called to live within the secular state or nation and that in the event of war a conflict of duties is inevitable, it should help them discover God's will, should honor their conscientious decisions, whether they are led to participate in or to abstain from war, and maintain with both alike the full fellowship of the body of Christ. It should call them to repent and to seek together that deliverance from the entangling evil which can be found in Christ alone.

The church must call its members to confess their share in the common guilt of mankind for the continuance of war and the spirit of war among the nations. Notwithstanding the notable efforts for peace which have been made within the church, clergy and laity alike have not done what they ought to have done to remove the causes of war by raising their voices against attitudes and policies making for war, and have not proclaimed with boldness the word of truth in time of war. Moreover they have often been guilty of greed, selfishness, distrust, and pride of race and nation, thus contributing to the embittering of relations among the nations. At the same time, the church must call its members to give "diligence to keep the unity of the Spirit in the bond of peace." Church members should earnestly strive to remove in their own lives every attitude and practice deriving from political, social and racial differences which are the seeds of war, and should seek the fruit of the Spirit, "love, joy, peace, long-suffering, kindness, goodness, faithfulness, meekness, self-control."

The church should remind its members that the principle of the unconditional supremacy of the state or nation, advanced either in time of peace or of war, is incompatible with the church's faith in Jesus Christ as its only Lord and is therefore unacceptable as the final norm of judgment or action. It is the church's duty to serve the nation in which it is placed, but the greatest service which it can render is to remain steadfast and loyal to its Lord and to test rigorously all claims of national interest by his gospel.

The church, confessing its faith in redemption through Jesus Christ, sees in every man a "brother for whom Christ died." In time of war, as in time of peace, it should pray not only for the nation in which God has placed it, but also for the enemies of that nation. If Christians in warring nations pray according to the pattern of prayer given by their Lord, they will not be "praying against" one another. The church should witness in word, in sacramental life and in action to the reality of the kingdom of God which transcends the world of nations. It should proclaim and obey the commandment of the Lord, "Love your enemies."

APPENDIX B
THE AMSTERDAM ASSEMBLY[1]
1948

Every man may serve the cause of peace, confident that—no matter what happens—he is neither lost nor futile, for the Lord God Omnipotent reigneth.

In this confidence we are one in proclaiming to all mankind:

I. WAR IS CONTRARY TO THE WILL OF GOD

War as a method of settling disputes is incompatible with the teaching and example of our Lord Jesus Christ. The part which war plays in our present international life is a sin against God and a degradation of man. We recognise that the problem of war raises especially acute issues for Christians to-day. Warfare has greatly changed. War is now total and every man and woman is called for mobilisation in war service. Moreover, the immense use of air forces and the discovery of atomic and other new weapons render widespread and indiscriminate destruction inherent in the whole conduct of modern war in a sense never experienced in past conflicts. In these circumstances the tradition of a just war, requiring a just cause and the use of just means, is now challenged. Law may require the sanction of force, but when war breaks out, force is used on a scale which tends to destroy the basis on which law exists.

Therefore the inescapable question arises: Can war now be an act of justice? We cannot answer this question unanimously, but three broad positions are maintained:

(1) There are those who hold that, even though entering a war may be a Christian's duty in particular circumstances, modern warfare, with its mass destruction, can never be an act of justice.

(2) In the absence of impartial supra-national institutions, there are those who hold that military action is the ultimate sanction of the rule of law, and that citizens must be distinctly taught that it is their duty to defend the law by force if necessary.

(3) Others, again, refuse military service of all kinds, convinced that an absolute witness against war and for peace is for them the will of God and they desire that the Church should speak to the same effect.

We must frankly acknowledge our deep sense of perplexity in face of these conflicting opinions, and urge upon all Christians the duty of wrestling continuously with the difficulties they raise and of praying humbly for God's guidance. We believe that there is a special call to theologians to consider the theological problems involved. In the meantime, the churches must continue to hold within their full fellowship all who sincerely profess such viewpoints as those set out above and are prepared to submit themselves to the will of God in the light of such guidance as may be vouchsafed to them.

On certain points of principle all are agreed. In the absence of any impartial agency for upholding justice, nations have gone to war in the belief that they were doing so. We hold that in international as in national life justice must be upheld. Nations must suppress their desire to save "face." This derives from pride, as unworthy as it is dangerous. The churches, for their part, have the duty of declaring those moral principles which obedience to God requires in war as in peace. They must not allow their spiritual and moral resources to be used by the state in war or in peace as a means of propagating an ideology or supporting a cause in which they cannot wholeheartedly concur. They must teach the duty of love and prayer for the enemy in time of war and of reconciliation between victor and vanquished after the war.

164

The churches must also attack the causes of war by promoting peaceful change and the pursuit of justice. They must stand for the maintenance of good faith and the honouring of the pledged word, resist the pretensions of imperialist power, promote the multilateral reduction of armaments, and combat indifference and despair in the face of the futility of war; they must point Christians to that spiritual resistance which grows from settled convictions widely held, themselves a powerful deterrent to war. A moral vacuum inevitably invites an aggressor.

We call upon the governments of those countries which were victors in the second world war to hasten the making of just peace treaties with defeated nations, allowing them to rebuild their political and economic systems for peaceful purposes; promptly to return prisoners of war to their homes; and to bring purges and trials for war crimes to a rapid end.

APPENDIX C
THE NATIONAL INTER-RELIGIOUS
CONFERENCE ON PEACE

In a press conference before the recent National Inter-Religious Conference on Peace held in Washington, D. C., Bishop John J. Wright took pains to emphasize that the meeting sought to deal with permanent questions of peace, not with specific crises. John Bennett's keynote address adhered in the main to this, although he seemed to know a good deal about the policies which alone can "undercut the paranoia of China" and judged that the United States now "exacerbates it . . . with everything that we do or leave undone." The second keynote address, by Rabbi Jacob V. Weinstein, departed altogether from Bishop Wright's reserve, and singled out for special criticism United States policy in Vietnam (*The New York Times,* March 16, 1966). Before the three-day conference was concluded, the reservation was of no effect.

In the interest of ecumenical ethics in this country, we should not be silent—to the contrary, the silence needs to be broken —about the fact that a great number of the Roman Catholic participants at this conference, and some of them long-time friends of the older ecumenical movement and knowledgeable about its teachings, felt that it was "insufferably self-righteous." Was this not because of the particularity aimed at in condemnations of political policy by some of the churchmen assembled? Also we ought not to be silent about the fact that an increasing number of Protestant churchmen feel the same way concerning specific pronouncements, having unavoidably the backing of their religious leaders, addressed to them, which they in conscience believe to be incorrect. These persons cannot properly be said to be "dropping out of dialogue."

The most important thing of all is that when we turn toward particularity we turn from deliberating fully upon a number of matters of extreme importance in the elaboration of a political ethics. John Bennett's keynote address at this conference was in the main a model of Christian address to the problems of war and peace.[1] This means that he limited himself to a forthright expression of "somewhat general statements" (to what Bishop Wright called "permanent questions") which, if taken seriously, would have profound impact upon political policies: e.g., "We should not use bombs, nuclear or conventional, against centers of population"; "resolve never to use nuclear weapons first." Around these and like propositions *deliberation* should center, in order for us to test whether we agree that these are entailments of Christian faith and practice in the politics of today's world.

But then in a brief paragraph Bennett yielded to the temptation that the conference and the churches and Christians should be more specific, because of his assessment of the urgent need that they provide a "corrective" to right-wing pressure upon the Administration. "If it is true that the President feels stronger pressure from those who would expand the war than he does from those who would restrict it or end it now, whatever else we may think about our policy in Vietnam, *we should be able to agree on our responsibility to counteract that pressure.*" This concedes that religion's voice need not even be the whole political truth, much less the whole of the Christian insights that need to be brought to bear upon policy dilemmas! We need only to seek to provide a counterweight either to present government policy or to identify pressures upon it in one direction or another. This would be to say that to tell a true prophet is to ask whether he prophesies against the government, or against the right wing!

Clearly this led away from examination of the general

167

premise at work in Bennett's proposal and upon which deliberation among Christians and all religious men should be focused,
in order for us in unity assembled to tell whether this is a
valid political judgment in today's world and/or entailed by
Christian perspectives in contemporary political and military
affairs. This was the premise that de-escalation is always the
lesser evil. If not, then recommendations to this effect in this
particular case may be correct or incorrect as a matter of
prudent, responsible political decision. Or perhaps Bennett's
proposal can be grounded in the proposition that the moderate
course is always the wiser—to be sustained in our government
policy by the cancelling out of extremes. Perhaps de-escalation
is always right, or the moderate course is always right. Then
and then only could Bennett's proposal have warrant, that
churchmen seek to be a corrective when they speak, and not
the church speaking in all that as such they say. There was,
finally, the astonishing assumption, obscured by the resolve
to reach a particular conclusion, that whatever else we may
think about the government's policy, about the alternatives,
about politics in general, or the views we hold about the light
our faith throws on the nature of politics, still the correctness
or adequacy of any of these things has little or nothing to do
with the soundness of a specific "agreement." Would this not
be to make a principle of doing right for the wrong reasons
(or at least from unexamined reasons, which if placed under
scrutiny might undergo such change that the agreement would
not be forthcoming)? Then how can one know the agreement
was sound?

NOTES

INTRODUCTION

1. See below, "The Church and the Magistrate."

2. The present writer has not the antipathy to "curia" that many people have; and I know that there need to be such persons and organization in and among the churches. The word is used for the habits, the modes and goals of operation, and the established practices in denominational and church council social action leadership that are seriously in need of rethinking and reform. A more neutral word for the leaders themselves would be "civil servants" of the churches. This supposes them to be open to such radical changes as may be needed, and indeed that they might take the lead in this.

3. See portions of the Oxford and Amsterdam Conference Reports printed among the Appendixes, and references thereto in the text below.

4. Professor Bennett disclaims any interest in perpetuating this phrase. In fact, "middle axiom" is, like "responsible society," a poor term. These expressions simply summarize an ecumenical consensus that once existed. They mark the point at which in ecumenical ethics we ceased to press on in fundamental analysis of the Christian undestanding of the social good (lest disagreement break out), and instead leaped over to policy-making pronouncements on which, it was found, churchmen could reach some sort of agreement.

5. *On Liberty* (Library of Liberal Arts; Indianapolis: The Bobbs-Merrill Co., 1956), pp. 43 ff.

WHO SPEAKS FOR THE CHURCH?

1. Meeting of the Central Committee of the WCC in Geneva, February 8, 1966, as reported the following day in *The New York Times.*

THE ABSTRACTNESS OF CONCRETE ADVICE

1. *Christianity and Crisis,* November 15, 1965.

2. Let me make it quite clear that journals of Christian opinion (like *The Christian Century, Christianity and Crisis,* and *Christianity Today*) and groups of Christians, clergy and lay, joined together to advance some specific cause they believe to be vital, are in an entirely different class from conferences sponsored by NCC and WCC. Even when the latter "speak only for themselves," they speak from a platform that engages the church and Christian social ethics more than do these journals of opinion or special voluntary groups acting upon church and society.

I will only observe that there impinges upon journals of Christian opinion a responsibility not to limit too much the range of specific opinion expressed in their columns; and also that they have a responsibility, while advancing particular causes and encouraging a wide range of debate, not to neglect to deepen and foster Christian understanding as such. On the latter point, a check of the articles with the notation "E" for Ethics in the annual index of some of these journals seems to indicate a degree of "cooperation" with the alleged providence of God in secularizing church and society.

Concerning groups of Christians banded together in behalf of specific political actions, I will only for myself express the view that there would be some virtue in devising a way of saying that the designation that they are "Christian" is "for purposes of identification only"—lest they impugn too much the conscientious prudential judgments of their fellow Christians who disagree with them in these particulars, and beyond warrant place Christian morality behind their specific causes. This view of mine doubtless arises from the fact that I am required in ever writing a "Letter to the Editor" *not* to use the name of Princeton University if I am expressing a citizen's opinion that is not within the area of any special competence that I may have.

3. In January, 1967, Hanoi seems to have moderated this position somewhat. It can be argued that this government now means "settlement in accordance with the program of the National Liberation Front," etc., to be placed on the agenda at the negotiations, once these are begun, along with other proposals to be discussed. Coupled with the demand that the bombing be "permanently and unconditionally" halted, however, the demand for final settlement in accord with Hanoi's four points would seem (for all practicable purposes) still to condition the opening of allegedly unconditional negotiations. So at least the statesman *may* have to view the matter, knowing the link between the exertion of

force and progress in negotiations. Not yet in this world is diplomacy a matter of "Come, let us reason together" about both our proposals. In these regards, Christians need to be as wise as serpents while harmless as doves! We should not try to keep up with the liberals on Manhattan Island as did Senator Jacob Javits when he came out for "unconditional" cessation of the bombing—and said it could later be resumed if acceptable negotiations did not follow (*The New York Times*, February 13, 1967). After Hanoi replied to the pope's latest peace appeal by renewing its demand for "definitive and unconditional" cessation of the bombing, the Vatican newspaper commented a day or so later that peace is not now possible in Vietnam. Senator Robert F. Kennedy continued to make domestic political capital out of this reply, because of the fact that the word "permanent" had been replaced by the word "definitive." This only shows that the pontiff knows how to read a diplomatic document better than the senator. Moreover, the senator surely knew that there are open channels by which President Johnson could find out or Hanoi could make clear whether any such construction was to be placed upon this wording, i.e., whether Hanoi meant to follow our "unconditional" cessation by "unconditioned" acts of de-escalation on its own part. Whereupon Hanoi made clear its unaltered demands for a negotiated victory in the South, or for negotiations under conditions that would likely lead to that, when it flaunted diplomacy by publishing the exchange of notes President Johnson had initiated at the beginning of the January pause. Had this not happened, one can imagine how "evident" it would now be to a great many American people that their President is acting in bad faith and does not want peace sincerely enough to see the shift of meaning from "permanent and unconditional" to "definitive and unconditional" cessation!

John M. Hightower of The Associated Press reported, in *The New York Times*, May 9, 1967, a four-month period of deep negotiation for peace initiated by the Polish government and revolving around a ten-point *Polish* summary of what the United States would be willing to talk about. Beginning as long ago as November, 1966, and proceeding through the bombing pauses in January, 1967, Mr. Janusz Lewandowski, chief Polish delegate on the International Control Commission, tried to mediate the conflict, acting through Ambassador Lodge. At one point, Mr. Hightower writes, President Johnson in attempting to open peace talks and scale down the war decided that "no responsive action was asked of North Vietnam." They were informed that "if they wished to make any move in any area of the war to curtail military operations, the United States would be alert and responsive." Hanoi ignored all this; and it was this, among many other feelers, that Ho Chi Minh flouted when he unilaterally published in March, 1967, the exchange of letters between himself and President Johnson. All the old demands for victory over the South Vietnamese—the "four points" as the "sole settlement"—have been repeated by Col. Ha Van Lau of North Vietnam at the so-called court sponsored by Bertrand Russell in Stockholm (*The New York Times,* May 9, 1967). In the face of all this, anyone who continues to demand that the President make peace *soon* should be asked in what respects his solution differs "definitively" from capitulation. He would seem not to be able to recognize a "tribunal of war," an "arbitrament of arms," when there must be one; or to know the nature of responsible negotiation on the part of this nation.

Finally, if we are talking about effecting any political purposes in South Vietnam, we ought not to forget the protraction of the negotiations for more than two years in the context of President Truman's goodwill gesture of stopping an offensive that (as it later became known) had the Chinese armies staggering in Korea. (See Bernard Brodie: "Morals and Strategy," *Worldview,* September, 1964, pp. 4-8.) Not yet is this a world in which the structures of a "just endurable" peace are apt to be agreed to by an undefeated opponent *under conditions of cease-fire.*

At least we Christians should not forget that a statesman cannot forget these things if he is trying to accomplish some purpose by the use of force. If, on the other hand, we are only proposing a face-saving way to extricate ourselves from the costs paid and exacted in accomplishing some political purpose in Southeast Asia, we should make this clear—and not disguise these opinions as the real conditions of choiceworthy negotiations that can secure the objectives of political stability in Southeast Asia or the self-determination of South Vietnam.

4. This is *not* the best reading of what was said at Geneva. See below, pp. 102-18. But is not this likely what was heard?

5. *World Conference on Church and Society: Official Report* (Geneva: World Council of Churches, 1967), Report of Section III: "Structures of International Cooperation—Living Together in Peace in a Pluralistic World Society," par. 95, with 44, 52, 94, and 97.

6. Because of the French and Russian vetoes in the Security Council, and because of the financial crisis of the UN leading to a likely curtailment of the initiative of the Assembly if the UN is not to be destroyed.

The "style" of Christian social ethics we are presently discussing may be described as "The Only Alternative and Other Possibilities."

Here is another example: How many churchmen and other Americans have in the past year condemned their government's actions in Vietnam while appealing to the reconvening of the Geneva Conference—knowing in their hearts that the Presidents of this conference (Russia and England) are as yet not going to reconvene it? Not even the détente between Prime Minister Wilson and Kosygin in February, 1967, has as yet maneuvered Russia into the politically efficacious position of being willing to take this initiative. Then we would still have to bring up the question whether France will agree to attend—before ever the Geneva Conference and its International Control Commission can be used to make new, enforceable peace arrangements in Vietnam.

7. "Structures of International Cooperation: Living Together in Peace in a Pluralistic World Society." Report of Section III, par. 101.

8. *Ibid.,* par. 92. This statement is a prime example of how to be led away from the "first essentials" of Christian moral judgments.

9. *Ibid.,* par. 108.

10. *Ibid.,* par. 93.

11. *Ibid.,* par. 92.

BETWEEN GENERALITY AND PARTICULARITY

1. Z. K. Matthews (ed.), *Responsible Government in a Revolutionary Age* (New York: Association Press, 1966), pp. 301-23.

2. See my "The Uses of Power," *Perkins School of Theology Journal,* Fall, 1964, pp. 13-24, and "The Ethics of Intervention," *The Review of Politics,* July, 1965, pp. 287-310.

3. Helmut Thielicke, *Theological Ethics* (Philadelphia: Fortress Press, 1966), I, p. xxi and other places.

THE CHURCH AND SOCIETY SYNDROME: THE GENEVA CONFERENCE

1. It is no answer, of course, to this criticism of the lack of decision makers from the executive heart of "the responsible society" to cite the presence of Congresswoman Edith Green among the United States participants, or Professor Byron Johnson's experience in government, or the distinguished gentleman, a lifelong student of the international system, who walked out of one of the sessions! My real point is to ask why, if church conferences are to continue to try to speak responsibly in specific terms to "the responsible society," there should not be on balance a greater proportion of Christian laymen from the middle echelons of executive departments where the crucial decisions are prepared.

2. The first such ritualistic utterance to come to my attention: "Geneva 1966 may have marked a turning point in ecumenical social thinking and social action. But unless its impulses are absorbed into the lives of the churches themselves, it could turn out to have been just one more way station in Christianity's slow descent into decay and extinction." Harvey Cox, "Geneva 1966," *Commonweal,* August 19, 1966. pp. 525-28 at 528.

3. To the end, very vocal opinions from the "South" and reticence from the "North," especially on the part of the Americans, in speaking to our fellow Christians from around the world the special responsibilities devolving upon Christians and churches in a country that has great power and commensurate political responsibilities seemed to me to be what too often passed for dialogue at this conference. Indeed, it is seriously proposed by some that as a methodological principle such imbalanced dialogue will be the shape given to proper ecumenical discussion by an adequate response on all our parts to what God is doing in the world.

4. "Man and Community in Changing Societies," Report of Section IV, par. 92.

5. *Ibid.,* par. 24.

6. "Structures of International Cooperation—Living Together in Peace in a Pluralistic Society," Report of Section III, par. 109.

7. *Ibid.,* par. 46.

8. Report of sub-section 3 to Section III, p. 3.

9. *Dialog,* V, Autumn, 1966, pp. 247-48.

10. Ed. by John Bennett (New York: Association Press, 1966).

11. I cannot agree with the statement made by Roger Shinn at the American Society of Christian Ethics, January, 1967, that Geneva demonstrated the death of neo-orthodoxy (and that he never attended a more cheerful wake). It was rather that rigorous reflection was emptied from the doing of neo-orthodox ethics.

12. "The Nature and Function of the State in a Revolutionary Age," Report of Section II, pars. 34 and 35.

13. It is no answer to this objection to say that a conference cannot be "open" on all sides at once, and that Geneva 1966 was designed to be open to dialogue with Marxism. We need to know in which direction primarily to be open if we wish to do Christian social ethics in an ecumenical age. The Second Vatican Council managed an "opening to the left" and even started a dialogue with atheism while still being primarily concerned that its formulations should, so far as possible at the present stage of Roman Catholic thought, build bridges to the Protestant, Anglican, and Orthodox worlds.

174

14. "Structures of International Cooperation—Living Together in Peace in a Pluralistic Society," Report of Section III, pars. 105-107.

15. International Edition, July 28, 1966.

16. The fact that the Vietnam conflict was not then negotiable, and the nature of the present tragic arbitrament of arms going on in that country as well as who continues to be adamant, was made clear by two statements in the news while we were in Geneva: (1) "We have repeated again and again our willingness to come to the conference table anywhere, any time, under any auspice, in order to bring the violence to an end. Again and again we have said that there is no bar to the inclusion of the Viet Cong in any such negotiation." Vice-President Hubert Humphrey, speaking at Texas Christian University, quoted in *The New York Herald Tribune,* Paris edition, July 16-17, 1966. (2) "Hanoi dismissed today all compromise proposals to bring about an end to the war in Vietnam. . . . An article in Nhan Dan, official organ, . . . asserted that its program was the 'only correct stand' and the 'sole basis' for settling the Vietnam problem. It said that the first point which demanded the withdrawal of all American troops, military personnel and weapons from Vietnam and cessation of all 'acts of war' by the U.S. against North Vietnam was 'particularly important.' This is the starting point and basis of the four points," the article stated. "This is the principle of principles to settle the Vietnam problem. . . ."

Of another point, acceptance of the political program of the South Vietnam National Liberation Front, the political arm of the Viet Cong, the article said this was the "only correct political program to settle the political affairs of the South Vietnamese people" (*The New York Times,* International Edition, July 25, 1966).

17. "Pastoral Constitution on the Church in the Modern World," par. 80, in *The Documents of Vatican II,* Walter M. Abbott, S.J., general editor (New York: Guild Press/America Press/Association Press, 1966).

18. Conference General Document No. 42, July 24, 1966.

19. The probability of this side effect of the dramatic dissent of Americans from their government's policy during wartime may be shown from a report in *The New York Times,* February 20, 1967. Proceeding from the *last* paragraph (where journalists put the background) on up to the *first* paragraph (the news event) and the headline, this news story reads as follows: On the occasion of the meetings and demonstrations in Washington, D.C., in late January 1967 by 2,000 Protestant, Roman Catholic and Jewish members of Clergy and Laymen Concerned About Vietnam, there

175

was conceived the idea of holding a Fast for Peace in Vietnam. The sponsorship of the fast was undertaken by the members and the minister of the Berea Presbyterian Church in St. Louis, the Rev. Carl S. Dudley. Their announcement was that from Feb. 9 to 11, 1967, over one million American Catholics, Protestants and Jews in 412 cities and 37 states held a three-day fast in protest against the "aggressive" war in Vietnam. "We may be challenged on these figures," said Mr. Dudley, "but we think we can back them up." Thereupon an article in the North Vietnamese official newspaper and its news broadcasts cited all this, and hailed the "condemnation of the United States aggressors seething throughout the world, including the United States," "the mounting struggle of the entire people of the United States of America against Johnson's aggressive war in Vietnam," and concluded that this was "proof that the Communists would win the war." The headline in the *Times* read: "Protest Rallies in U.S. Buoy Hanoi."

This is not recounted to discourage dissent, but to show that there is no such thing as a "witnessing" action in behalf of or against a specific political *policy* that is not also a political *action*. In politics there are no mere gestures. The doers of every political action must count both the costs and the benefits to flow from their actions. Neither our bombardiers over Vietnam nor protestors fasting for peace can escape the obligation to estimate also the side effects of their actions, the innocent lives taken "beside" their intention, and all the indirect costs as well as the possible direct benefits of what they are doing. No religiously or morally motivated action specifically intervening in politics escapes from the test of prudence or a proportioning of probable good against the probable bad effects of the action put forth.

20. Bishop B. Julian Smith, Bishop Prince Taylor, the Rt. Rev. J. Brooke Mosley, Dr. John C. Bennett, Mrs. Edith Green, Dr. Kenneth Boulding, Miss Charlotte Anne Bunch, and Dr. Byron L. Johnson.

21. *Christianity and Crisis,* July 12, 1965.

22. This was said to be "consistent" with the resolutions of the General Board of the NCC adopted in Madison, Wisconsin, December, 1965, and in St. Louis, Missouri, February, 1966—which resolutions were, indeed, less judicious in arriving at a balanced set of specifics than the WCC statement of February 16, 1966, and therefore in seemingly less need of subsequently acknowledging our government's willingness if there are two to make peace.

23. Whether they do so or not, or do so correctly, is another matter. The point is that councils and delegations of churchmen no

matter how able they are, or how many facts they gather, *cannot* do this; they cannot supplant the office of political prudence.

24. Since it can be safely said that the caliber of the economists assembled at Geneva was most striking of all the professional groups, this says something to us about whether the church can be the church competent to speak in particularity on specific issues by the use of experts. Someone has to pick the experts; and so no apostolate of experts can give the churches such voice.

25. "Structures of International Cooperation—Living Together in a Pluralistic World Society." Report of Section III, pars. 94 and 95.

26. *Ibid.,* par. 17.

27. We shall have to continue to use this *Geneva* expression, but I do not find the "lesser evil" warrant used in the report of the 1948 Amsterdam Conference. This report certainly stated that "we are one in proclaiming to all mankind: war is contrary to the will of God. . . . The part which war plays in our present international life is a sin against God and a degradation of man" (*The First Assembly of the World Council of Churches,* ed. by W. A. Visser 't Hooft. New York: Harper and Bros., 1949, p. 89). But in answer to the question: Can war now be an act of justice? The three positions were: pacifism, military action as the ultimate sanction of "the rule of law" in a world without impartial supranational institutions, and a third position (placed first in the sequence) described as follows: "There are those who hold that, even though entering a war may be a Christian's duty in particular circumstances, modern warfare, with its mass destruction, can never be an act of justice." This is an affirmation principally about modern warfare that is close to what we call today "nuclear pacifism." The exception concerning a Christian's duty, even so, to enter war in particular circumstances might be construed by some to entail a particular "lesser evil" judgment; but the statement does not use this language.

It is evident that the statement concerning Christian participation in war adopted by the 1948 Amsterdam Conference was powerfully affected by the Bishop of Chichester's eloquent statement, in the discussions of the assembly, in support of the proposition that "modern war . . . cannot be an act of justice" (*Ibid.,* p. 102). In these discussions, Mr. LeQuesne suggested the inclusion of the following words (which grammatically somewhat resemble the wording which Geneva attributes to Amsterdam): "There are those who hold that modern warfare with its mass destruction can never be an act of justice, but of those some hold, while others would deny, that to enter into a war may be a Christian's duty in particular circumstances" (*Ibid.*, p. 103). At the request of the chairman, this suggestion was left to the drafting committee for reconsideration. The result was the formulation (quoted above) which subordinated the exception, "even though entering a war may be a Christian's duty in particular circumstances," to the general assertion that "modern war, with its mass destruction, can never be an act of justice." How it can ever be a Christian's duty to do something that can never be an act of justice (or is contrary to the will of God), we are never told. But neither Mr. LeQuesne nor the final report sought to explain this by adopting the language of "the lesser evil."

The 1937 Oxford Conference on Church and Society was the one that in its "three main positions which are sincerely and conscientiously held by Christians" included one clearly based on justice; but neither does it speak of "lesser evil" (*The Oxford Conference,* ed. by J. H. Oldham. Chicago: Willett, Clark and Co., 1937, pp. 162-67). However, the Oxford Report does speak of "the best that is possible" falling short of the glory of God, and as being in that sense "sinful"; and it affirmed that "to do what appears as *relatively best* is an absolute duty before God, and to fail in this is to incur positive guilt" (*ibid.*, pp. 162-63, italics added). That is as close as either conference came to "lesser evil" language. Moreover, the relatively more positive language of the "relatively best" came in the preamble, and does not seem to be controlling in the definition of three possible Christian positions on the matter of participation in war which Oxford then went on to outline. The "relatively best" went along with war as one of the "marks of a world to which the church is charged to proclaim the gospel of redemption." This was not used as a main way to delineate a Christian line of action. What happened after Oxford was that "sin" and the "relatively best" as permanent (theological) "marks" of our world came more and more to be moralized.

The pertinent sections from the 1937 Oxford Conference and the 1948 Amsterdam Conference are printed in Appendixes A and B below. They deserve careful study. From Oxford to Amsterdam there was a decline in appeals to justice as a warrant; but does this mean an increase of "lesser evil"? It looks as if the singular emphasis upon "lesser evil" in recent, especially American, discussions of participation in war has not its foundation in ecumenical ethics before the Geneva Conference.

28. If not in this instance, by now in the course of his large contribution to ecumenical ethics, John Bennett must be quoting himself in citing previous teachings, even as Vermeersch quoted himself in his own moral theology when he cited large sections

of the papal encyclical *Casti connubii* which he himself wrote. My point here is simply that ecumenical ethics cannot be a thing apart, with a life of its own made out of weaving together a continuity among statements that have been issued with those about to be issued. All possible theological work has also to be taken into account if we are to have any community of discourse in the doing of Christian social ethics at and between ecumenical conferences.

29. To put Oxford and Amsterdam together.

30. "Pastoral Constitution on the Church in the Modern World," par. 80, in *The Documents of Vatican II*.

31. Surely a much more apt *Christian* characterization than the 1948 Amsterdam statement that "war is contrary to the will of God" was the one given by the 1937 Oxford Conference: "War, the occasions of war, and all situations which conceal the fact of conflict under the guise of outward peace, are marks of a world to which the church is charged to proclaim the gospel of redemption" (J. H. Oldham, ed.: *The Oxford Conference*. Chicago: Willett, Clark and Co., 1937, p. 162). But these are *not* the ethico-political characterizations of war that are needed in doing Christian political ethics.

32. I am suggesting, in effect, that ecumenical ethics needs to return to Oxford and begin again. That was by far the best of these statements of Christian ethics on the question of war. At the same time, it may be observed that the process of decline from statements about justice was a process of increasing use of what I have called statements of moral fact. All that I have said about Geneva's "Nuclear war is the greatest of evils" can be said of Amsterdam's "Modern warfare, with its mass destruction, can never be an act of justice." Given a correct characterization* of that "mass destruction" restrictive upon the meaning of modern warfare, that statement is as correct as Geneva's, but only given the correct characterization, and with the omission of the commas to change this from a nonrestrictive to a restricted description of the sort of war that Amsterdam meant to condemn. However, the point here is that the particularity of this expression, and the failure to unpack principle from factual verdict, is already driving out justice from ecumenical consideration in connection with the war question, and on the way to bringing in "the lesser evil." That, plus the indubitable pressure of the contradiction between having declared to all mankind that war is sinful and "contrary to the will of God" and searching thereafter to find warrants for a Christian ever to participiate in it. See also Appendixes A and B.

179

33. Perhaps I should report that I, who was at Geneva as "co-opted staff," i.e., by WCC invitation, made a mild attempt to speak on the floor in this plenary session, which was held early in the conference. Then in the final session when the report and conclusions on international relations were under discussion, at the point of the Vietnam resolution I sent M. M. Thomas a genial note which simply said that if another point of view from the United States was wanted, it looked as if there was nothing else he could do but recognize me (under the rule that observers, staff, etc., could speak if the chair called upon them). This is mentioned only as a last minor point in the legislative history of that conclusion; and concerning whether this was or could have been a deliberative body in making these conclusions its own. The pressure of time was such that if I had been M. M. Thomas I wouldn't have recognized me either. Upon the participants, early in the subsection meetings and within the limits allowed even them by the structure of the conference, rested the responsibility for the input in discussion; and, as we have seen, with regard to the Vietnam conclusion it was its passage intact that from first to last was uppermost, or rather was the only way for the conference to speak with one voice *specifically*. Dialogue was better in the corridors and at the Hôtel Intercontinental.

34. No doubt this was the reason the Vatican Council did not make the "clear statement on this matter" for which Gollwitzer criticized it.

35. The United Presbyterian Church's Confession of 1967 seeks to express in the matter of several social questions how God's transforming *reconciliation* ought to be confessed in action. The effect of bringing "reconciliation" too directly to bear on questions of war and peace, or the effect of a Christomonistic theology lacking a sufficiently articulated doctrine of the orders of creation and of sin, and the effect of having a theory of politics *not* based on the latter also, is shown in this Confession's call for "the pursuit of fresh and responsible relations across every line of conflict even at some risk to national security." The words "at some risk" do not have a plain meaning in regard to questions of security. Of course, the awesome aspect of political leadership and action is that there are always risks. There is always some risk; indeed, more than some risk. But political responsibility cannot possibly include weighing the real options and then choosing one that has greater risks than another to national security. Being imprudent is *not* a duty of political office. One might imagine in future years, if this Confession is taken seriously, it being said that it may not be safe to have a Presbyterian in the White House if he is a *good* Presbyterian!

Instead, the relevance of reconciliation to the responsibilities of political office has to do with the always urgent task of effecting a *greater coincidence* between the national interests and the interests of other peoples. This has bearing upon alertness to ways in which the structures may be changed so that, consistent with national security, a greater actual reconciliation and identification, which in politics passes not from man to man, might pass through them. When, for example, the evangelical church in West Germany opened and broadened public debate in that country by calling attention to the fact that Germany should at the most opportune moment accept the *de facto* boundaries and give up all claim to the eastern territories, this was not a proposal to introduce Christian abandonment directly into politics. Nothing would be abandoned except an aggravating claim. This was not to risk national security, but to *enhance* it while at the same time contributing to the actual reconciliation and stability of middle Europe on which that security depends. There might have been, we shall see, a more responsible way for the evangelical church in West Germany to act to open debate on that government's policy toward the eastern European communist countries. This would have been to pronounce: "If in order to recognize officially Germany's *de facto* eastern frontiers it should be necessary for the Bonn government also to do 'X,' this will not fail to be supported by a large body of Christian opinion in our country." Here "X" stands for any possible connected cost or for another policy decision tied with the one recommended which the government might have to make at the same time.

A PROVISIONAL MODEL FOR SPECIFIC POLITICAL PRONOUNCEMENTS

1. Statement made by the Archbishop of Canterbury during the debate on Rhodesia at the forty-seventh Meeting of the British Council of Churches, October 26, 1965.

2. This seems to be the viewpoint which Richard Goodwin—a "Kennedy man"—would personally espouse. He, however, did not give equal weight and prominence to this connected alternative when contending against the bombing in the North and the present level of the war in South Vietnam, in his article, "The Lengthening Shadow of War," *Christianity and Crisis,* October 31, 1966, pp. 235-40.

3. The members of the delegation from the Philippines with whom I talked at Geneva were quite agitated concerning the Vietnam "conclusion." "Our government has just decided to send several thousand troops to Vietnam," they said (but not in plenary), adding: "We are only one hour flying time from China—*one hour!*"

181

4. Seymour Topping reported in *The New York Times,* August 21, 1966, that Indonesia and Malaysia, upon bringing their "confrontation" to an end (and thus releasing British soldiers for the first time from their long and lonely efforts to defend Malaysia against subversive disintegration), have now established a joint defense against communist guerrilla operations that are threatening and in actual operation against both countries. He also reported that a similar cooperative effort between Thailand and Malaysia has begun against the Peking-based Thailand Patriotic Front—which launched the guerrilla operations assaulting southern Thailand near the Malayan border.

Can there be a Christian perception of the fact that it would be a lesser evil if American involvement in South Vietnam were brought to an end, but on principle no Christian perception of the fact that a prompt United States presence in support of these Indonesia-Malaysia-Thai efforts to resist subversive assault may be warranted? If we can call for a specific peace at its specific price, can we not call for specific military involvement at its specific costs? Cannot our conferences say: "If the President finds it necessary to use force to aid these countries in their efforts to defend themselves, he will not find himself forsaken by Christian opinion"?

5. It was not hard to get below the surface of the Indian agreement with what the conference said on Vietnam (and below their understandable feeling that nonalignment is the only possible course for India) to see that one of the basic reasons for this on the part of these participants (including Mr.Thampy, who was a member of the committee that drafted the statement) was their conviction that the United States is wasting in South Vietnam strength and resources that may be needed in India. The Indian government at the present moment is having to divert *one half* of its total budget from the vast social and economic needs of their country to military defense along the border with China.

6. Illustration 3 is introduced, despite its generality, because illustration 2 may be too specific for Christians to want to think through at our conferences—once we adopted the responsibility-inducing language I am suggesting should be the form of specific recommendations if these are going to continue to be made. On the question of the necessity of an effective American military presence in Asia, see M. M. Thomas' "The Fears and the Futility" in *Dialog,* Winter, 1967, pp. 30-33.

7. On illustrations 4 and 5: The nation that has adequate conventional force to bring to bear, not the one that does not, is the nation that *can* (as anything more than a "declaratory" policy or ritual performance) *renounce* the use of nuclear weapons or renounce

first use, i.e., begin to take seriously the Geneva statement on nuclear war. There seems to be less actual capability for conventional defense, less possibility of flexible, graduated response in the European theater than there was two years ago, and therefore more, not less, danger nuclears would be used. Ten years from now (or is it three or five years?) mainland China can and probably will renounce the use of nuclear weapons, or first use, *and mean it,* i.e., be *able* to mean it because of China's huge standing army. If Geneva's weighty moral condemnation of nuclear war is meant seriously to open a great debate on that subject, the alternatives have also to be called soberly to the attention of everyone, Christians and non-Christians alike.

8. Such was the reasoning of Dr. Albert Wohlstetter of the University of Chicago (*The New York Times,* February 13, 1967), who incidentally is a member of the Board of the Council on Religion and International Affairs. His reasoning goes against *my* moral grain and against as well my judgments of prudence. But in the absence of clear Christian warrants, how could some future conference of churchmen fault his conscience or wisdom by majority vote? Our role should rather be to stop short of *or* to hold open this range of policy options.

TOWARD AN ECUMENICAL ETHICS

1. Of even the pre-Geneva preparatory study volume *Christian Social Ethics in a Changing World* (ed. John C. Bennett; New York: Association Press, 1966), Daniel Day Williams said in a review: "It is fair to say that the essays appear stronger on the critical than on the constructive side. To say this is in part simply to recognize the difficulty of the task of Christian ethics today. But it also may point to the danger of a contextual ethic in dismissing the traditional search for ethical principles as an outworn and futile quest. It is not clear to me how we can talk about 'humanization' as an ethical norm without having some way of exploring, defining, and interpreting the nature of man, his relationship to history and to nature, and the forms of human relationship in which human values are realized. What happens in many of these essays is that familiar Christian principles of the dignity, freedom, and equality of man reappear in new form, only they are not recognized principles. . . . It may further be remarked that one major gap in this discussion is the lack of attention to the common law and the forms of constitutional guarantees of human liberties in the Western democratic tradition. Granted all this now has to be judged in a new setting, but surely we are not to discard the values achieved in centuries of exploration of the legal process in a free society. A

183

theological interpretation of law is badly needed today" (in *Social Action* and *Social Progress,* January-February, 1966, p. 49).

2. *The New York Times,* June 30, 1966.

3. "Pastoral Constitution on the Church in the Modern World," par. 76, in *The Documents of Vatican II.* Numbers in parentheses in the text above refer to official paragraphs of the Constitution. Italics sometimes added.

4. See Appendix C.

5. Concerning "theological prefaces," it may not be inappropriate for me to introduce several personal experiences of what I must judge to be insufficient deliberation before speech or action, or insufficient concern for the task of strengthening Christian ethical understanding and upholding a Christian ethos among us.

I was the scribe for a small group of theologians assembled to draw up the first draft of a theological position or background paper and of the statement later issued on contraception by the General Board of the NCC, February 23, 1961. Because this was to be the first such statement from so high an agency of the ecumenical churches in this country, and because of the deep theological-ethical issues in this matter, I asked why the theological statement could not be integrated with the particular pronouncement planned to be issued, so that both could be deliberated upon, improved or corrected by the councils above our committee, and both be addressed together to the churches and to the world. No, the pronouncement had to be of a certain length, brief and precise. To any one who wanted it the theological-ethical "background" would be made available. It could not even be discovered whether there was any body or official in the NCC organization to whom my proposal might be addressed and from whom could be secured an answer to the question whether this might not be an improvement in the deliberations of those who were about to speak. So far as I have subsequently been able to discover, there is in the NCC no permanent organ for procedural self-criticism and reform, although at big meetings there is an agenda committee. Yet it cannot be denied that in general it is deliberation in Christian terms and spreading this abroad, and not specific permissions or prohibitions, that is most lacking in the formulation of sex and marriage ethics today, as this is done by individual professionals or by church groups, precisely in an era when we are coming in touch with Roman Catholic ecumenism, whose main trouble in this area is the *rigidity* of its traditional formulations.

During the years I have been a member of the NCC's Commission on the Church and Economic Life, many an excellent position paper has been produced upon economic questions, contributing to the general education of the public and of churchmen and to my own enlightenment. Still, it cannot be denied that in all this little advancement has been made in relevant Christian ethical statement, or that the whole effect of our recent theological revival was simply to impose upon particular pronouncements the necessity of beginning with a brief, thin theological-ethical preface. It would be better if we forthrightly committed ourselves to the task of general "adult education" as one of the tasks of the churches in our society. This is no way for the church or Christians as such to speak, and it is therefore no way for them to speak to the churches and to the world.

I know little of the internal reorganization that has recently been instituted in the NCC, except for participating in a group called together to advise the new Commission on Educational Development (under which the department on family life has been placed) on how it should best proceed. It seemed to me then that the reorganization must have been based on some scramble principle—on the principle that, since everything is related to everything else, we should in this age of "worldly Christianity" abolish all the former divisions and categories of Christian ethical knowledge (such as marriage and the family) and expect our ecclesiastical "civil servants" to be Renaissance men uniting all knowledge in the leadership they give to the churches. It seemed clear that there was only one theological premise behind the reorganization and designed to be the one way we now do ecumenical Christian ethics, namely contextualism. As was said of the Geneva report on "Theological Issues in Social Ethics," if the way we are set up to deliberate about Christian social ethics is contextual, there will be nothing at all surprising if the resulting ethical decisions are only contextual. If not before, Christians should get ready to ask whether, for example, sufficient Christian ethical reflection or profound enough deliberation went into the position favoring abortion that, I venture to predict, will soon be reached.

[Since the above paragraph was written, the New York State Council of Churches and the Protestant Council of the City of New York have announced their support of the pending bill to "liberalize" the state's abortion laws (*The New York Times*, December 13, 1966). Without calling that conclusion wrong, one may well wonder where the persons making this decision received their theological-ethical instruction. This is a genuine question, and not a rhetorical one, since so far as I know no American Protestant theologian has given sustained attention to this issue. And the two outstanding contemporary Protestant moralists who have investigated the ethical and religious issues bearing on abortion would quite certainly be opposed to many of the provisions of the proposed statute, and as

185

adamantly opposed to the reasons and the view of life advanced in behalf of this "reform" as any Roman Catholic. (See Karl Barth, *Church Dogmatics,* III/4, ¶ 55: "The Protection of Life," pp. 414-23, and Helmut Thielicke, *The Ethics of Sex,* pp. 226-47.) The question, therefore, which clamors for an answer is whether this decision by the city and state councils of churches was based on any defensibly Christian line of reasoning, or was instead a socio-medical proposal for dealing with grave human problems by *absolutizing* an unscriptural distinction between the respect and protections due to be given to conscious and to nascent life. This darkness and that light are both alike to God in his deliberations and dealings with humankind.]

My Princeton colleagues William M. Beaney and Edward N. Beiser, in a review of political proposals and action that followed the United States Supreme Court's decisions striking prayer and devotional Bible readings from the public schools gave an impressive account of the effective counteraction mounted largely by the NCC department of religious liberty and headed by Dean M. Kelly in defeating the Becker Amendment which by constitutional means would have corrected the court's recent line of decisions ("Prayer and Politics: The Impact of Engel and Schempp on the Political Process," *Journal of Public Law,* Vol. 13, No. 2 [1964], 475-503). In the same issue of the same journal I showed (I believe) at least that up to that point insufficient deliberation had been mounted by the churches concerning the separation of church and state, concerning the consequences of the passage of that amendment not for the comparatively trivial matter of school prayer but upon other far more important assaults upon the general religious foundations of our culture that are perfectly consistent with religious liberty, and entirely constitutional until the recent quite questionable bias of the court ("How Shall We Sing the Lord's Song in a Pluralistic Land?" *ibid.,* pp. 353-400). We acted, I think, before we thought enough as churches, specifically opposing the action of some of our legislators to initiate a measure, again quite constitutionally, to call a halt to the court's overrulings of some of the main aspects of American life. It is a prediction already fulfilled to say that some people would then say that secularization is something *God* is doing!

6. This statement, taken alone, is far too individualistic. It has to be balanced by all that is said in these recent Catholic documents concerning "social justice and social charity" and the expressly articulated action-relevant principles or analysis entailed in this.

7. Paul Ramsey, "The Vatican Council on Modern War," published concurrently by *Theological Studies,* June, 1966, and *Theology Today,* July, 1966.

8. *Social Action,* April, 1965, p. 10.

9. "Structure of International Cooperation—Living Together in a Pluralistic World Society," Report of Section III, par. 91(d). Moreover, the drafting committee subordinated this reference to Christians working within the existing order and conflated it with the previous paragraph about "the witness of non-conformity."

10. The only positive statement made in the Geneva report concerning the vocation of military service had to do with the function of the army in "nation-building" ("The Nature and Function of the State in a Revolutionary Age," Report of Section II, pars. 58-61). This cut across our "Western" constitutional assumptions that the army should always be separate from civilian affairs and subordinate to the civil authority. This was good medicine for Americans to hear, in face of our ordinary assumption that the military can never be the force representing the traditions of a people and their development, and in face of the widespread opinion that American dealings with military regimes must always be wrong. But this was no substitute for a clear recognition of military service in its relation to the justice already politically embodied among peoples that have achieved nationhood. This has to be said even if until now in this aeon the military serves "justices" that do not agree.

11. See the remark of Professor John H. Hallowell: "Politics is unlike engineering in that it is a form not of technology but of moral endeavor. It is concerned not with *making* something but with *doing* something. As one writer put it: 'We do not build the state to live *in* (as we live in a house)—we live the state. Our living state is an integral part of our lives. Here, the builders are what they build'" ("The Nature of Government in a Free Society," in Z. K. Matthews, ed. *Responsible Government in a Revolutionary Age.* New York: Association Press, 1966, p. 185). It is a fundamental flaw in much of our current ecumenical ethics that it is so largely a product of "technical reason"; this goes along with our propensity for policy-making exercises.

12. *Social Action and Social Progress,* January-February, 1966, pp. 34-45.

13. *Ibid.,* p. 44.

14. *Ibid.,* p. 43.

15. *Christian Social Ethics in a Changing World,* ed. by John C. Bennett; *Responsible Government in a Revolutionary Age,* ed. by Z. K. Matthews; *Economic Growth in a World Perspective,* ed. by Denys Munby; *Man in Community,* ed. by Egbert de Vries. New York: The Association Press, 1966.

16. See note 5, above.

17. Faith and Order Trends: Two Weeks at Aarhus. National Council of Churches, September, 1964, p. 4.

18. Perhaps the problem of getting apt procedures for ecumenical deliberation and study is an incorrigible one. Perhaps I look upon the modes of operation in "Faith and Order" with rose-colored glasses, or the eyes of an outsider.

In any case, the reader should be informed that one competent participant at the 1963 Montreal Conference was moved to substantially the same judgment upon it as I have been forced to render upon the 1966 Geneva conference. "Few could feel that the product of the drafting group," J. Robert Nelson wrote, "was as good as any one man by himself, in consultation with others, could have written. And worse, the pressure to write papers deprived the delegates of time to discuss the four major reports of the theological commissions, which had worked for nearly a decade in preparation for Montreal." Despite the plans that the conference have "sufficient freedom from 'hustle' of every kind to encourage sustained efforts to penetrate the main issues," Nelson notes, these plans were derailed and "the ponderous paper-producing processes of Lund, Evanston, and New Delhi proved to be inevitable also at Montreal." He concluded, rather too hopefully, that "if the Lund conference of 1952 marked the end of comparative ecclesiology, Montreal ended the series of attempts to deal with a variety of massive theological issues in the context of excessive organization and frenetic activity" ("Critic's Corner," *Theology Today*, October, 1963, pp. 412-14).

Still, from a derailed railroad car one can tell something about where it was going! One should not forget the theological commissions at work for nearly ten years in preparation for Montreal, nor fail to notice the shift from "comparative ecclesiology" to "massive theological issues" in the ecumenical research sponsored by "Faith and Order." There needs to be a similar shift in the aspired goals of "Church and Society" from "comparative policy making" to the fundamental issues of Christians social ethics, even if the procedural difficulties continue to derail us.

THE CHURCH AND THE MAGISTRATE

1. Reprinted, with the permission of the editor, from *Christianity and Crisis*, June 28, 1965, pp. 136-40.

2. Some readers may recall that I protested this surface unanimity of vocal liberal religious opinion during the campaign itself ("Is God Mute in the Goldwater Candidacy?" *Christianity and Crisis*, September 21, 1964, pp. 175-78).

More to the point in evaluating the worth or justifiability of invoking in this context the authority, which is denied them in other contexts, of "the opinions of church bodies on particular issues," it should be noticed that only belatedly was the distinction between these particular opinions and "basic Christian convictions that bind a member of his church" used to heal the wounds of some sincere churchmen who were in anguish because it seemed to them that a solid phalanx of church pronouncements had been used to deny them legitimate disagreement. To them *Christianity and Crisis* made the proper reply; but apparently this journal has nothing to say to Mr. Barry Goldwater himself, who in a recent letter asked plaintively: "Now that the presidential campaign of 1964 is far behind us, I should like to know the basis you used in an editorial which said I had set myself 'against the overwhelming consensus of Christian so-cial doctrine enunciated by the churches'" (*Christianity and Crisis,* July 25, 1966, pp. 179-80). This letter thus began plaintively, but it ended on a note of injured self-righteousness. This is at least an understandable response in view of the self-righteousness that will always be *attributable* to a consensus religious ethics that in trying to enforce its particular conclusions does not specifically and at length call attention to the fact that Christians and other reasonable men may legitimately disagree on specific matters. The editor simply noted "Mr. Goldwater's letter is published here as a courtesy to him," and did not trouble to give him the proper reply, about the basic convictions that bind a Christian and those that do not. To have drawn attention to this distinction would have brought to mind the fact that earlier it had been forgotten.

APPENDIX A

1. *Official Report,* ed. by J. H. Oldham (Chicago and New York: Willett, Clark & Co., 1937), pp. 162-67. The Oxford Report is now readily available in *Foundations of Ecumenical Social Thought* (Philadelphia: Fortress Press, 1966).

APPENDIX B

1. *The First Assembly of the World Council of Churches: Official Reports,* ed. by W. A. Visser 't Hooft (New York: Harper and Bros., 1949), pp. 89-90.

APPENDIX C

1. "The Issue of Peace: The Voice of Religion," *Worldview,* April, 1966, p. 6.

PREVIOUS BOOKS BY DR. RAMSEY

Basic Christian Ethics
Christian Ethics and the Sit-In
War and the Christian Conscience
Nine Modern Moralists
Deeds and Rules in Christian Ethics

BOOKS EDITED BY DR. RAMSEY

Freedom of the Will (Jonathan Edwards)
Faith and Ethics: The Theology of H. Richard Niebuhr
Religion: Humanistic Scholarship in America